JOURNEY INTO NATURE

A *Spiritual Adventure*

Michael J. Roads

H J Kramer Inc
Tiburon, California

H J Kramer Inc
P.O. Box 1082
Tiburon, CA 94920

Library of Congress Cataloging in Publication Data

Roads, Michael J.
    Journey into nature: a spiritual adventure/Michael J. Roads.
      p.   cm.
    ISBN 0-915811-19-7 : $10.95
    1. New Age Movement. 2. Nature—Religious aspects.
3. Consciousness—Religious aspects. 4. Pan (Greek deity).
I. Title.
BP605.N48R615   1990
291.2'12—dc20   89-80727
                                                              CIP
                                                              r89

Editor: Suzanne Lipsett
Cover art: Kinsley Jarrett
Cover design: Spectra Media
Editorial Assistant: Nancy Carleton
Book Production: Schuettge and Carleton
Typesetting: Classic Typography
Manufactured in the United States of America
10 9 8 7 6 5 4 3 2 1

To my beloved Treenie.
We are not alone in the fairy ring.

To Our Readers

The books we publish are our contribution to an emerging world based on cooperation rather than on competition, on affirmation of the human spirit rather than on self-doubt, and on the certainty that all humanity is connected. Our goal is to touch as many lives as possible with a message of hope for a better world.

Hal and Linda Kramer, Publishers

Acknowledgments

A s always, I extend my thanks to my wife, Treenie. It is not easy to summarize the countless ways in which a loving soul mate can support a struggling spouse, but this is what Treenie does for me—constantly. Very simply, she is there—there when I need her, there when I think I don't. Through everything, always and forever there!

My sincere thanks to Hal and Linda Kramer. Together, they have not only helped me reach the true audience for my literary efforts, but have become part of Treenie's and my life.

Life has a way of producing the right person at the right time. Greg Armstrong became the catalyst for turning my metaphysical reality into print. I thought the timing had not yet arrived, but his intensity and passion convinced me otherwise. Greg, from my heart, thank you for releasing the genie from the bottle!

I would also like to thank my editor, Suzanne Lipsett. I understand that this was not an easy manuscript to edit; however, it was a challenge she met. If I have managed to clearly communicate all I have tried to say, then Suzanne's skill has proved invaluable.

Acknowledgments

I owe thanks to our four children, too. Throughout their years of growth, they have all left impressions of value, as they continue to do today: Duncan—volatile, high powered, catalytic; Adrian—silent, enigmatic, strong in purpose; Russell—sensitive, adventure seeking, vulnerable; and Tracy—the other woman in my life, a bud awaiting bloom.

One of the most important parts of a book is the cover. The inspired art work on this cover is the result of my good friend Kinsley Jarrett seeing true. This book is a response to an inner journey. Equally, Kinsley's inner journey revealed what he drew. What a perfect combination! Thanks, Kinsley.

My sincere thanks also to Dan Millman. Unbeknown to him, his inspiration helped me open the Door.

Contents

Author's Note

This book is complete, but it is also a sequel to my last book, *Talking With Nature*. In order to enter a deeper relationship with Nature, I was required to become a participant *with* Nature rather than continue in the role of an onlooker. I did not find this at all easy. I was propelled into a metaphysical reality, a reality I did not enter willingly. Yet on the inner levels I had already made a commitment. Let's just say I didn't know I had! We humans are like that. We come to this planet with a clearly defined destiny, but as soon as we take on human form, we forget it. Life then carries us kicking and screaming toward our perfect goal while we try our hardest to abort the mission.

Nature is a force of immense power, so my pathetic struggles were like those of an ant aswim in an ocean. It was not long before I gave myself willingly to the force carrying me, opening myself to a hidden Nature of boundless metaphysical proportions.

This book explores the connectedness of all life. I have learned that separation is a lie. To me, this means that I, the writer, and you, the reader, connect in consciousness as we share these pages together. We are not separate in consciousness, just individual. The journey of self-realization I unwittingly undertook revealed an inner dimension of Nature, a dimension beneath the surface of our everyday reality that is of immeasurable value to us, though we have long been conditioned to deny its existence.

I offer this book as a means of igniting your own inner awakening and laying bare the lie of old, worn-out beliefs and concepts. Becoming awake is the birth of purpose.

Michael J. Roads
Queensland, Australia
April 1989

1
Meeting a Myth

Treenie let go of my hand as we paused while crossing over the low wooden bridge. It was a primitive-looking affair, but built in such a way that it had survived the regular powerful floods that had often engulfed it. The sides were no more than logs bolted onto the structure. They allowed a clear view of the water as it flowed beneath our feet while they served as a convenient seat on which to contemplate the beauty.

"Look." I looked at the river where my wife pointed. The water was crystal clear. There, sitting bold and dominant in about six feet of water, was a large stone shaped like an egg.

"That's odd," I said. "Because the water is so clear, sunlight has caused algae to grow over the river stones . . . all except that one."

Together, we peered through the distorting water at the stone. The day was glorious and the midwinter air crisp and cool, even here in our subtropical valley. We had been walking for exercise and fun, listening to bird songs as we strode down the country lane. Wild lemons, guava, and lantana jostled for space over the road, the flowers of the lantana nodding in a gentle breeze as we passed them by. Butterflies hovered among the yellow, pink, and red flowers, not caring that winter weather should forbid such activities, while the courtship of tiny wrens among the foliage suggested an early spring.

"Perhaps it's meant for us." Treenie's voice was soft as she stared at the stone. I glanced at her. "You don't expect me to leap into this freezing cold river, do you? Not for a stone?"

Treenie smiled without replying. She knew me well enough to know I would break ice to go in if I really wanted to.

"Why don't you ask the stone if it wants to be with us?" she suggested.

"Why don't you?" I countered.

"Oh, come on. You're the one who talks to rivers and rocks. Now's your chance to make a new friend," she teased. I stared down at the stone, intrigued not only by its strangeness in the river but by an energy I could feel emanating from it. "Okay, stone," I said. "How about it? Do you want to come home with me?" I spoke with some mockery in my voice, but the words that poured into my mind came with such force and authority that I instantly sobered.

"I have waited a long, long time in many rivers and in many places. Although I belong to no one, right now I belong with you."

I gazed at the stone in surprise. Although I had expected to hear an inner response, the content and implication caught me off guard. While Treenie watched with resigned amusement, I stripped down to my shorts and, with some trepidation, waded into the river. Ugh! It was cold. The moment I was waist deep in the water, a car trundled across the bridge. Several faces stared out at me as if I were mad!

I knew there was no way I could retrieve a rugby-ball-sized stone without getting soaked, so I plunged beneath the water and dived for the vague, distorted shape beneath me.

I grabbed and lunged for the surface, but the stone resisted. It was heavy! I took a deep breath, shivered, and revised my strategy. This time I dived, grabbed, braced, lifted, and then scrambled underwater to the nearest bank. I took a grateful gulp of air as my head emerged from the river. Back on the bridge, I dried quickly in the warm sun before pulling on my clothes. Then, cradling the heavy stone in my arms, I continued walking homeward with Treenie— somewhat slower than before.

For the next year, the stone remained basically silent. I learned that it required irregular immersions in a bucket of fresh water—it would demand these in no uncertain terms. But apart from that, all the stone offered was the puzzle of its existence. On one occasion when it was issuing a fine stream of bubbles in a bucket of water, I asked if it had a name or a purpose. The answer was ambiguous, to say the least.

"I am a Guidestone—your Guidestone—and you are my purpose. It was you who programmed me for an event such as this."

I frowned in puzzlement. "What do you mean?" I asked. "What event? What is a Guidestone? How could I program you?"

"In the bud of innocence awaits the bloom of truth." I waited for more, but that was it! A fine stream of bubbles silently popping at the surface of the water was the stone's final comment.

How I detest riddles!

A few months later, Treenie and I were in Brisbane, where I was giving a "Talking With Nature" workshop. The event was well organized, and the room was more than big enough for the forty people involved. I spoke of my love for Nature, of our connection with the Earth, and of our loss as we become alienated from Nature. I shared my view of the Spirit of Nature and of how, by building a new relationship with Nature, we can transform ourselves. I suggested that we are not separate from Nature but a constructive intelligence within it, and that by our actions or misactions we connect or separate ourselves from Nature. The response from the people involved was rich and warm.

Following a shared lunch, the afternoon session commenced. I felt apprehensive, for I had no set format and was about to embark on what seemed a foolish experiment. A few days earlier, the Guidestone had emerged from a lengthy silence to tell me I should give it a twelve-hour soaking in water followed by twelve hours in full sun. This would, in effect, charge the stone with energy. The Guidestone then instructed me to take it with me to the workshop and place it within a circle of the participants.

I had arranged the seating to form a horseshoe, with me seated in the open space. Following my intuition, I began by asking each person to look across the half circle into the eyes of a person opposite. Why I suggested this I did not know, but the impulse was so strong I followed it. A time of surrender resulted as we lowered the barriers between us by making eye contact. We became vulnerable in our defenselessness, and unexpectedly, steadily, the energy in the room climbed as we surrendered our personal privacy.

When the energy had become comfortable, I stepped into the center, lifted the Guidestone from its bag, and placed it on the floor for all to see. Until this moment, the stone had been hidden. Now, as I rolled it into view, forty pairs of eyes fastened onto it.

With electric suddenness, the energy in the room leaped higher. I suggested that each person focus on the stone, seeing it in a new way. "View it as energy rather than a stone," I said, "and allow that energy access to your Being." Then I sat down.

To say I was surprised by what was happening is putting it mildly. One could almost cut the energy in the room, it had become so potent. I decided I would not become involved but rather would keep an eye on things from the sidelines. In full innocence, I stared curiously at the Guidestone, aware of its power. That's strange, I thought. I have never noticed that little hole in the large end of the stone before. I leaned forward to see better, gripping the arms of my chair. I could clearly see a tiny hole about the size of a mustard seed. I stared at it, frowning in consternation. I had studied the stone in minute detail and before that moment would have sworn there was no such hole.

As I stared, all normality came to an abrupt and sudden end. Without warning, my body locked. I could not move a finger. My arms and legs were frozen, immobile; I couldn't even blink. With this horrifying realization, sweat broke out all over me, but in the same moment I was drawn from my body as though I were smoke and sucked into the tiny hole in the Guidestone.

I begin to experience a duality of awareness I have never known before. My conscious awareness is with the psychic essence taking human shape within a vast chamber in the center of the Guidestone, yet I am also conscious of my helpless physical body in the workshop room.

As I become aware of myself in the immense chamber, I begin to tremble. All space seems to be filled with pure, raw, seething energy, terrifyingly impersonal. The chamber is filled with what appears to be fire, yet I sense extreme heat and icy cold simultaneously. Energies of incomprehensible dimensions fuse as the shattering power of this colossal dynamism roars and surges in a silent crescendo of sound. All around me, echoing over and over, up and down the scale of sound, one word reverberates incessantly—*run, run, run, run, run, run, run* . . . —endlessly repeated with mind-shattering power. I stand transfixed, weak, and helpless while the words of this Energy blast into me.

"You stand at the center of the Stone, the microcosm of the macrocosm. You stand at the center of the Universe."

I am frightened. What the hell am I doing here? How did I get here? I want out. I desperately want to follow the shattering command I am hearing over and over and run as far and as fast as I can, but I cannot unlock my physical body!

In a tiny voice I ask, "Why am I here? How did this happen?" Nothing! I might as well have sung "Waltzing Matilda" for all the good it does me.

"I am the Keeper of the Door." The voice fills the entire chamber, echoing through my consciousness with immense power. There is only one response I can make. "What door?"

"If you cannot find the Door, then it has no place in your consciousness."

Standing dwarfed in this huge chamber, surrounded by and engulfed in surging power beyond anything in my ability to comprehend, I have never felt so alone, so totally vulnerable.

Without warning, I suddenly know I am *not* alone! In a moment of revelation, I know that life has conspired to arrange this moment of truth. Certain key people have been drawn almost against their will to attend this workshop. In some way I am linked to every person in this room. It's a perfect cosmic setup! I, who had created a framework in which the others could be participants, have been cast into a participation beyond my wildest dreams. I know with absolute certainty that if I fail in whatever it is I face, it will be a long, long time before I have another opportunity.

I am encouraged, and for the first time since entering and taking human form in the Guidestone's mystical chamber, I attempt to move, to walk forward. Immediately, the Energy, the Keeper of the Door, surges and boils around me, determined to frustrate my efforts, while the pounding command—*run, run, run*—erodes my will. I can only compare the experience to walking into a heatless, raging white fire while pushing underwater against the density and might of a raging river. Each trembling step is an exercise of will. Each takes all my reserves in strength and effort, drawn from both my metaphysical—beyond the physical—and physical bodies.

Meanwhile, my body in the chair is still rigid and my eyes still stare at the Guidestone. Sweat and tears mingle on my cheeks. I am aware of acute embarrassment, a sense of utter disbelief.

Ages seem to pass while, with huge effort, as though burdened by massive weight, I manage, step by ponderously slow step, to creep farther into the chamber. Throughout this seemingly endless time, the Keeper of the Door roars and hurtles, filling all time, all space.

Startled, I see before me a pair of massive doors. They fill the whole chamber, disappearing from view on either side and far above. I gape at them with sinking heart. Nobody could open such doors. It is not humanly possible. There are not even any handles, nothing except doors of a size and apparent weight beyond reckoning. I am very close now. Summoning all my remaining strength, I take one more faltering step against the hostile power of the Energy.

I can touch the Doors.

Strength surges in me. Immediately, all around me, the powerful, insistent, will-shattering command echoes and reverbcrates with awful intensity—*run, run, run...*—and I quail before it. Again I try to flee, but my uncooperative physical body remains locked, eyes fastened to the Guidestone. I cannot run.

Summoning all my will power, I slowly struggle to raise my arms until I can place one hand on each Door, where they meet in a hairline crack before me.

At that precise moment, in my locked physical body, a

dull pain explodes in the top of my head. I can feel the pain as a strange throbbing intensity, as though the crown of my head is somehow opening and closing to an alien rhythm.

Standing small and weak before the mighty Doors, I gather all my remaining strength and will power, ready for one huge final effort.

"Stop!"

The command is such an onslaught of sheer power that all else fades before it. I stop!

"To open the Door is to invoke an awesome responsibility. Do not open the Door unless you are prepared to accept this."

The weak part of me tries once more to run, but a silent whisper — *Stay, do not break* — holds strong. Defiantly, without the faintest idea of what I am letting myself in for, I shout as loud as I am able into the silence of a mystic world, "I can . . . and I will!" and I push, as hard as I can, against the Doors.

There is no resistance. The Doors fly open as though they had the weight of gossamer, and I stand on the threshold of another world. It is a familiar world, yet new and different.

Spinning in silent orbit, a new Earth awaits. With a vision defying normal eyesight, I can see into a valley, both familiar and containing a sense of order beyond human experience. Three-dimensional life coexists within some other dimension, causing all substance and form to be illumined. An inner radiance shines forth as outer reality. Even as I stare at this beautiful, wild yet peaceful Nature, the valley fills the space beyond the Door and a sense of expectancy fills me.

10

The invitation is crystal clear.

I have the opportunity to enter this new reality. This is the Earth of some other age, home to a sensitive, loving humanity. Standing in the Doorway, gazing with exaltation, I know I must step through.

Once again, with unbelievable power, the words from the Keeper of the Door pour into me.

"If you step into the Beyond, the full force of Nature shall pivot in your being. Can you accept this enormous responsibility?"

Behind me, faintly now, the echoing *"run, run, run"* continues, but it no longer holds the power to control me. With the vision of a new Earth before me, I hear my own voice clearly reply with power and authority. "I can accept this responsibility and use it with wisdom."

My thoughts, however, are rather different. Did I say that? What am I letting myself in for? What's going on? Help!

"Remember! The full force of Nature. Misused, it will destroy you."

With these words, all resistance from the Keeper of the Door fades.

Before me, a new Earth awaits my footsteps. I am exhilarated . . . and exhausted, purposeful . . . and scared!

I attempt to step forward one pace, but find it impossible to make any progress. Some strange, invisible membrane seems to be between me and that new Earth, and try as I may I cannot walk through. It resists me as easily as if I had tried to walk through invisible glass. Half a dozen times I attempt to force my way through but without success. I even try punching the invisible barrier, but this has about as much effect as punching a pillow.

Finally, I stand back, puzzled and defeated. "All that effort for nothing," I mutter. "It's ridiculous."

"Oh, I wouldn't say that. I didn't expect you would get this far. I certainly don't expect you to step through the Door."

Shocked, I spin around. The person, or Being, I face smiles at me calmly. I step back hastily, away from the deceptive Doorway and the newcomer.

"Good grief! Who are you?"

Two disconcerting eyes look into mine, holding me in a gaze I cannot break. I stare in appalled fascination. There is no white to those eyes. The irises, considerably larger than those in human eyes, are a deep golden color containing flecks of intensely sparkling light. And the calm intelligence in those eyes is beyond anything I have ever encountered. Strangely, as he — it? — holds my gaze, I can feel my fear evaporating. Whatever this being is, violence is not part of it. I relax with a sigh.

"You ask who I am, yet you know. I have seen the answer within you."

The Being is considerably taller than I and I must gaze up at him. "I . . . I do?"

He nods absently, now looking through the Doorway. "Think about it. Take your time." He chuckles at some private joke. "Time is irrelevant here."

I stare at him, no longer feeling threatened. That he is human, or humanoid, is beyond question. He stands on normal legs, clothed in a pair of faded green denims. His bare feet are longer than normal, and his toes taper almost to a point. Even though he is clothed in a loose, faded green cotton T-shirt, an exceptionally well-proportioned upper body testifies to his humanness. His skin is the color of pale golden honey, not unusual in our multiracial society, but with his face and head all human normality ends. His large, faintly slanted eyes are set in a face of Oriental features. He has very high, fine cheekbones and a thin, narrow nose perfectly proportioned to his broad face. His lips are moderately full and clearly defined. On his chin is a tuft of fine downy hair too sparse to hide the fact that the chin itself tapers out to a blunt point.

Sensitivity and strength are contained in that face. It is fierce yet gentle, mellow yet wild and free. But the real challenge is above the eyes!

His eyebrows are no more than a thin line, and just above them small spiraled horns curve gently outwards. His skull is a bald golden dome. I have the impression that this dome is the repository of experience and knowledge far beyond anything conceivable in human terms, and that we humans are all as children by comparison. The bulge and expanse of forehead is greater than any I have ever seen, yet it is his ears that now hold my attention. They are not animal, but neither are they human. The ears are no larger than ours where they join the head, but from there they sweep back three times the normal length, tapering to an upper point covered in the same downy hair as that on the chin.

An incredible face. Totally beautiful, utterly serene. Just drinking in the detail of his features fills me with peace.

And then I know! I know exactly who this Being is.

13

"Pan!" I gasp the name aloud, and he smiles as our eyes meet. "But how? Why? What am I doing here?" I stutter to a halt, overfull of questions.

"You did not think your relationship with Nature could continue merely on a verbal level, did you? When you elected to jump into the river of life, you invoked certain forces that have long lain dormant."

He holds my gaze once more with a level stare that I am unable to escape. Not that I want to. I could willingly drown in his eyes, so compelling are they.

"Consider the experience you have just undergone," he continues. "What has begun here is your initiation into a different level of relating to Nature, but I stress it is only a beginning. You were unable to walk through the final barrier. As I introduce you to the inner world of Nature, you will find you are on a journey of discovery. Not only will you discover a whole *new* meaning to Nature, but within Nature you will have the potential to discover your Self. You may find the true Self of your Being. Only then may you pass safely through the Door. That membrane is your security, for what lies beyond the Door may be gained only through perfect timing. You *are* that timing. This is your path and your destiny."

"So what do I do now?"

"You open yourself to new experiences and willingly become involved in them. You began all this a long, long time ago. To enter a new reality of Nature, you must first experience Nature. Experience it as it *is*, and experience it not as an onlooker but as a participant. The mineral, vegetable, and animal kingdoms are part of the human Being. You must experience your own inner connections with these kingdoms. In this way, the knowledge and experience that are now buried deep in your psyche will become your conscious reality."

He smiles at me in a way that seems disconcertingly sympathetic. "I will help you. That is why I am here in the Guidestone."

I feel hopelessly inadequate. Compared to Pan — is it *really* Pan? — I feel that everything is far beyond me. And I am aware of a sudden, overwhelming fatigue.

Obviously, Pan is aware of my exhaustion, too. Concern flickers in his eyes. "Go now," he commands and clicks two of the long, tapering fingers of a strong, slender hand.

Instantly, all my awareness was focused on my physical body as I regained conscious control. I could again move my limbs and wipe away my sweat and tears. Now an emotional battle began, for I wanted nothing more than to collapse in a heap on the floor and sob.

The top of my head throbbed incessantly. I felt very fragile. Cautiously, I glanced around, expecting every eye to be fixed on me in curious speculation, but no one was aware of what had happened. I was astonished. I had been in the Guidestone for ages. A glance at my watch revealed that scarcely twenty minutes had passed. I placed a trembling hand on the top of my head, trying to hold it all together, when my eye caught Treenie's. The look in her eyes told me she knew that something had happened, even if she did not know what.

Somehow—I'll never know quite how—I survived the next hour. I listened while people shared their experiences with the Guidestone, and I became aware that several people realized that something fairly dramatic had happened to me. In all probability, they had been the crucial human element—consciousness—that had supported me when I had most needed help. I did not share my experience; to do so would have been beyond me. I was in emotional shock. Later I learned that a participant who was a close friend went away with a headache that lasted nearly three weeks. He swore he would never attend another one of my workshops!

As time distanced me from the experience, my acceptance of it, I am not proud to admit, rapidly diminished. After all, who in his right mind believes in Pan? My education had revealed him only as the mythical God of Nature with a human upper body and the legs and feet of a goat, and until this experience I had never had cause to question this description. But the Pan I met was far more than merely human, and totally unbestial. In the past, when sitting by the river listening to its silent—yet audible!—communication, I had often surmised that things might possibly go deeper than they appeared. My involvement with a metaphysical Nature continually required that I surrender much that is considered normal. But never in my wildest dreams had I expected anything like Pan. And yet it made sense. If Nature were intending to lead me deeper into its mystical consciousness, who would be a better guide than Pan, the god of this inner realm? The difficulty with this logical summary was that Pan himself was not logical. He was an affront, a challenge, to my cozy belief system, which I thought had already been stretched to its limit. That was my problem—the idea of Pan as my guide made sense, yet it was nonsense!

Curiosity caused me to try summoning Pan, even though I found it difficult to believe in him. How could I meet him again? How was I supposed to pass that final membrane by finding my Self? My journey into Nature up to now had offered me words and several rather unusual interactions with a river, but Pan was obviously the forerunner of extraordinary things. Should I just wait, or what?

I discussed the whole episode at length with Treenie, and she found it easy to accept. But that did not help me resolve the personal dilemma I was facing. Just to make matters more complicated, that little hole in the large end of the Guidestone simply was not there. I checked the stone carefully, and the hole did not exist. So how could I have been sucked into it? All that remained were impossibilities and questions!

A few months later, I received a letter from a man named Kinsley Jarrett. I had been receiving a trickle of letters in response to the recent release of my book *Talking With Nature*, and Kinsley's letter was among them. He had responded deeply to certain incidents described in the book and wanted to meet Treenie and me. Liking the tone of

17

his letter, I agreed to a meeting. As luck would have it, he and his wife, Valma, lived only a few hours away.

In due course, the Jarretts arrived at our home. What ensued was one of those meetings with strangers that are really the renewals of old friendships. After the first hesitations had been eased away, Kinsley asked if we would like to see the drawings he had done of various Nature Spirits. He had been a commercial illustrator, he told me. I felt skeptical, though, at the idea that Nature Spirits had appeared and remained present while he drew them. However, I hid this feeling as he took the first of his illustrations from the folder. Then I simply stared in fascination and awe. That Kinsley saw true I had no doubt. The detail and energy of his art leaped off the pages. Nature came alive in his work, vital and very, very real.

He laid a few more of his sketches before us and then, after hesitating briefly, brought out one more. A chill ran down my spine. It was Pan! As Kinsley had drawn him, an enigmatic smile played over Pan's lips. Once I looked into the eyes on the paper, I could not pull my gaze away. For perhaps ten minutes, I held that sketch of Pan's head and shoulders, drinking it in. It was accurate in practically every detail. Kinsley explained how and where he had seen Pan, but I hardly listened. All my denials of the Guidestone experience lay in tatters at my feet while Pan smiled mockingly at me from a simple sheet of paper.

No more than a week after Kinsley and Valma had departed, a tube arrived by post from Kinsley containing a rolled up picture. As I unrolled it, I knew that Pan was back to haunt me. A brief note explained that when Kinsley went back to his favorite forest nook he saw Pan there once more, and Pan had suggested that Kinsley make an illustration for me. I put the picture in a frame and hung it above my desk. I quickly found that no matter where I stood in the room, Pan's eyes were gazing into mine.

After that, I waited for something else to happen but nothing did, at least nothing like what I had anticipated.

An old friend from our past, Wendy, came to visit Treenie and me for a few days, and we had a lot of talking and reminiscing to catch up on. Eventually, responding to her questions, I began to discuss certain aspects of my relationship with Nature, becoming rather intense as we moved into my favorite subject. I noticed alarm on Wendy's face as she looked at me, but I dismissed it. Suddenly, she sat bolt upright, the alarm replaced by astonishment. "Michael! Stop! Your ears!" She paused in acute embarrassment, then forged ahead. "Your ears! They've grown long and . . . weird." She pointed at them. "While you were talking, they were growing. Even your face changed."

I ran my fingers over my ears. They felt the same to me! Wendy jumped to her feet, very agitated. "I must go outside," she said. "I need to get away for a few minutes."

Treenie and I looked at each other. "Well?" I asked. "Can you see weird ears, or is she imagining things?"

Even before Treenie could reply, I was on my way to the nearest mirror. I stared hard at my reflection, twisting my head from side to side. For one brief, heart-stopping moment, I saw Pan, his smile a mocking enigma as our eyes met. Then he was gone, and my own face reflected my bewilderment. Shaken but satisfied that my ears were normal, I returned to the room. Later, when Wendy had joined us, she explained how she had seen my face gradually change. Obviously, the change had not been physical, but something that seemed imposed upon my features.

It was considerably later when Wendy noticed the picture of Pan above my desk. "That's the face; that's it!" she exclaimed excitedly.

As though that were not enough, other people saw similar shifts in my physical being—five more times. Each time, it was the ears or face of Pan superimposed upon mine that drew their attention.

One day when I glanced at the picture of Pan, I clearly heard his silent question.

"Yes," I murmured aloud to him. "I do accept you now. I don't seem to have much choice!"

2
Becoming Water

Winter had ended. The sun shone on the river with unabated power, early morning shadows having retreated into thickets of trees and bush. Instead of diving into the inviting river, I slid into the water silently, for I wanted to sneak up on some water dragons that I knew frequented the riverbank to bask in the hot sun.

I scanned the dead, water-logged branches ahead of me, watching for the single movement that would betray the dragon's outline. Suddenly, it happened. With a slight pulse of a throat, the whole reptile became visible. Slowly, I moved closer, trying not to blink. Movement was effortless, for the water supported me as I gradually closed the distance. Finally, I was within six feet of the ancient creature, but I knew it was aware of my presence. For five, maybe ten minutes, we remained motionless.

A shoal of small striped fish began to feed on the debris I had disturbed in the shallow water. It was not long before they progressed from this to pulling on the separate hairs of my chest and legs, tugging with frantic energy in an attempt to detach their prizes. They tickled, and as I shifted slightly ripples of alarm radiated across the water's surface. Instantly, from a branch before me, an eighteen-inch water dragon leaped into the safety of the reeds. I gasped! I had not even noticed this particular dragon, yet it had been even closer than the one on which my gaze was fixed. Its skin rough, with corrugated, broken shades of gray, the reptile had blended perfectly with the branch. Yet once seen, the creature was clearly visible.

From the river came silent words: "You see yet you do not see."

It was true. The startled dragon had been in my full vision, yet I had not seen it. Now, because of the unnatural position of my head, my neck was aching, so I decided to end the game by creeping forward, closer and closer to the dragon statue. Five feet, four feet, three feet—explosive action. One bound and it, too, vanished into the dense waterside undergrowth.

I smiled in childlike satisfaction. In my own way and in my own time, I loved being part of Nature. Taking a deep breath, I slid underwater, swimming silently down into a deep, murky hole close by. I knew a large eel lived there, secure in its water world, believing itself to be king of its domain. And it probably was! Living under a submerged log, it fed on the hapless young perch that came within reach of its snapping, teeth-filled jaws. I saw the eel's hazy, bulky, sinuous outline and reached out to stroke it, but it had other ideas. As a six-foot-long, thick ropy shadow, it glided over my body, its velvet-soft skin cool as it slid across my belly.

I took another breath of air and dived again, changing direction. Now I allowed the underwater current to carry me as I drifted effortlessly, silent in body and mind, across the sunlit shallows of gravel and smooth river stones. Here I had to be more watchful, for the sluggish bullrout stung with the sustained touch of a red-hot knife. A flicker of movement ahead caused me to reach out, hanging onto an extra-large and convenient river stone.

Without alarm, eight fat river mullet were feeding on furry, dark green algae growing on the stones, their sleek, silver-gray bodies twisting and flashing as they grazed. These river mullet seldom ventured into the estuaries or ocean, probably preferring the comparative safety of the upper freshwater rivers. These fish were fat indeed, about a foot long and gleaming with health. I popped my head above water and, taking a really deep breath, let go of the stone to dive once more and drift among the flashing silver fish. There was no panic, no real disturbance. As a shoal, they swam around me, within reach, all the while twisting and rolling as they leisurely grazed their underwater pastures. I called to them in the silence of my mind, asking them to share their wisdom, but I heard nothing.

For a while I continued downriver, swimming deeper now in the water and occasionally surfacing for air. Disturbed, a large water tortoise raced vigorously ahead of me, and I playfully grabbed it as it clawed frantically at the water. Again, I popped to the surface, holding the struggling captive before me. Water dripped, while its legs continued to swing in the air and its snake head wove aimlessly back and forth. Gently I touched it beneath its mouth to feel the tiny, thin barbels protruding from its lower jaw, when to my utter astonishment it bit me! For a few seconds the tortoise remained attached, unaware of the pitfalls of hanging on! Then I plunged hand and tortoise beneath the water. Instantly, the tortoise let go, to disappear into the depths with determined and frenzied haste. I looked at my dented fingertip, smiling. Cheeky!

Quietly, I swam back upriver, easing my way over the shelves of submerged rock. Contented by the sun and lazing in that wonderful flow of living water, I reflected on my gradually strengthening bond with Nature. As a child I had been angry—not with an anger that other people had been aware of but with one that had simmered within me. I had had to endure a decade of being a very nonintellectual, nonacademic right-brained boy in a very intellectual and academically left-brain–oriented school. Not understanding why I was such a misfit, I turned to Nature. By tranquil ponds and in places such as Byron's Pool Woods, I found acceptance and refuge. My bonding with Nature happened in silence. Alone, I had nothing to say, so I learned early that rarest of gifts—to listen—not to people, but to Nature. I viewed people with distrust. That much school had taught me.

Eventually, my schooling ended and I began to work on my father's farm. At this stage, my relationship with Nature came under threat, for as a trainee farmer I was required to subdue Nature. Farming and Nature, I learned, were in direct conflict. I had to change, and my childhood connection with Nature became submerged, but throughout those years of farming it remained within me, a spark awaiting its time.

In my midtwenties, married to Treenie and with two boys, I emigrated with my family to Australia. Settling with them on the island state of Tasmania, I once again began farming, simply because I had no training in anything else and I loved the outdoor life. Over the next eleven years, I developed a new relationship with Nature. I learned of a potential bonding between a human Being and Nature, but there was a catch. Such a bonding had to be *experienced*, not merely conceived mentally. While the bond remained a concept, it was no more than speculation: it had to be actualized, lived.

Now all Treenie and I came to know was work, work, and more work. Sixteen hours a day were normal for us — up at 5 A.M. to milk the cows and feed the pigs and calves, breakfast at 9 A.M., then do a full day's work and end at 4 P.M. with the whole milking routine again. Day in, day out, such was the schedule every day for eight years. My love for Nature was buried under the sheer necessity of work.

But gradually, below the day-to-day routine, I was surrendering to the moving force of Nature. I was learning that to make a true connection with Nature — beyond the mind, beyond knowledge — I had to release the farm and open myself to Nature's metaphysical realms. Nature revealed to me that within the moment there is a movement that can be experienced as though one is attuned to the heartbeat of the universe. In this movement, there is Silence, and within this Silence is Wisdom.

In our decade on Tasmania, I made enormous changes in my thinking, becoming one of the foremost organic farmers on that tiny island state. Still, much more was needed if I was to enter the mystical kingdoms of Nature, and I wanted to do so with an intense, unabated longing. I felt that my true home lay in the heart of Nature. It was this longing, this deep inner need of mine, that took Treenie and me away from farming, now with three boys and a daughter, to travel around Australia in a kombi-type vehicle and a pop-top caravan.

After many adventures, we initiated a community project, and with about twenty other people went to live on a 345-acre property that was to become known as the Homeland Foundation Community. It was there I had to face myself—not an easy task! I learned that I took an aggressive attitude toward people, but that hidden behind this shield were the unresolved fears of a little boy. Throughout this four-year adventure, if there was conflict in the community, I would be in the thick of it. If there was confrontation, I would be there.

With some shock, I learned that the reason I did not like other people was that I did not like myself. Once I faced that fact, I could begin to solve the problem. It would be difficult to exaggerate the pain and trauma of coming to terms with myself. As I lowered my barricade of aggression, there was no shortage of people who would cut me to the quick in my vulnerability. I was a target, for I had been one of the most dominant in the community and was now defenseless. I cried more during this process than I had ever cried in my life. I allowed a little boy to cry. Many times I sat by the river in my mental and emotional pain and vowed that I would leave tomorrow. But tomorrow had a habit of never coming. Slowly and painfully, I learned that my greatest strengths were a handicap, were defenses, while within my vulnerability lay a seed of unrecognized strength. This was not an aggressive strength but a strength that revealed a totality within myself.

Had either Treenie or I known of the trauma we would have to face in that community, I doubt that we would have had the courage to enter it in the first place, for even Treenie did not emerge unscathed. She faced her own personal problems and suffered greatly as she let go of old patterns of thought and behavior. But like me, Treenie triumphed.

When Treenie and I left Homeland to settle a few miles away in the same valley, I had come genuinely to like myself. My growth as a human Being no longer depended on interaction with other people. When you can finally live in a community of forty people without conflict, you have found a measure of inner confidence and tolerance. Even my relationship with Treenie had taken on a new meaning. Before living in the community, we had been close, rather like two powerful vines entwined around each other, each offering and receiving support, but the community life had torn us painfully apart. As we each found our own strengths and inner capacities, we came back together, but in a different way. We were now individuals standing side by side, two strong, separate trees. Our support for each other was based on a new level of self-respect and love, and in a wonderful, magical synthesis of souls, the two of us experienced a new kind of love within our marriage. We bonded on a level of love and acceptance we had not attained in our first eighteen years of marriage.

Living by the river, my relationship with Nature grew anew. I was no longer turning to Nature as a refuge from people; now, once again, Nature was my teacher, and Treenie had become my Nature companion. Before our time at Homeland, Treenie had always seemed outside my journey into the inner realms of Nature, but now she was involved, and in some inexplicable way my experiences served as stepping stones in her own path. If, during one of my communications with Nature, I learned something new and profound, when I shared it with Treenie she had already experienced it, but on an entirely intuitive level.

As I swam in the river on that delicious spring day, I knew that the journey into Nature I had longed for was becoming a reality. Now I needed to find new levels of openness and acceptance, for already I was threatened by the sheer impossibility of Pan. Pan had told me I was to experience the inner kingdoms of Nature—the plant, mineral, and animal kingdoms—but I had a feeling there was more to it than that. Though I have a strong mystical side to my character, my strong logical mind was going to cause me trouble. How could I trust Pan as my guide if at times I still doubted his existence?

A light breeze had sprung up while I floated with my thoughts, dispersing them among the newborn ripples. Idly, I glanced around; then I recoiled in shock. Sitting cross-legged on the surface of the river close by was Pan. "Oh! You startled me!" I exclaimed.

He smiled, those incredible eyes holding mine. I wanted to ask him how he could sit on the water, but under that gaze all words dried up.

"We are going to begin now by stretching you. Let go of restrictive belief systems and all you consider normal and flow with what I offer. You alone will determine how your experiences within Nature will evolve. I am not going to tell you of what lies ahead, for you would build inner defenses against the unusual and unintentionally devise ways of reducing the impact of the unexpected. This would negate our purpose."

He paused while I digested his words. An intensity had built around him, and I could feel it within me, bringing clarity and quick understanding.

"If we are to bring about a transformation, then I must use the weapons of surprise to bypass your natural defenses to the unknown." He chuckled. "Such defenses are well developed in humanity; that is why the unknown is so vast. You must become changed, not modified. A metal that is forged into a plate one day and melted and reforged into a vase the next is not changed. Its shape is simply modified. However, if by some process that metal is transmuted and becomes gold, this is change. This is your inner purpose . . . to become changed."

"Er . . . what to?"

"That I cannot tell you. You have to *be* it to know." He became silent and I did some more digesting. I knew I was under his influence, for otherwise I would have felt far more agitated than I did.

"Let go," his voice coaxed me, the words echoing and reverberating in my skull. I struggled as my senses reeled.

"Let go." It is a command I cannot ignore. I feel my Self being drawn from my physical body, and I watch in helpless anguish as it slowly sinks beneath the water.

"I . . . I'll drown. I'll lose my body."

"No. A natural preservation will take place. Watch."

I watch as my body rises to the surface on its own volition and the mouth opens to take in air. The body is animated, even though I am no longer in it.

"You are alive; thus your body lives. Your purpose now is not to die and lose your body, but to experience aspects of Nature that are denied to the physical senses. The body is a unique vehicle. It will survive because you will survive." He pauses, and when he says the next bit I wish he hadn't.

"Of course, if you die to this physical reality, then your body will no longer accommodate you. Surrender your will to that which *is* and go with the experience. By letting go, you are safe; by resisting, you may create adversity. Flow with the water . . . and experience."

It crosses my mind to protest, but the thought dies unfinished. I no longer relate to a *me*. I am pure water—yet more. I both flow in the river that contains me and hover as an invisible mist above it. I no longer experience through eyes or ears. I perceive. I am a liquid that fills every part of the Earth. I can feel the consciousness of the Earth, the rhythm of its breath. I flow among the dense particles of solid rock, knowing the rock's consciousness. I am all puddles, ponds, lakes, and oceans.

No longer an isolated entity, I flow in savage splendor down rocky ravines, laughing as the sound of torrential, thundering water bounces and echoes from the rocks. I

31

lie in calm tranquility in icy, land-locked lakes containing the fish that swim in my sluggish depths. I am rain falling from the skies, and, frozen, I fall as snow.

As a muddy swirl, I flow toward the sea, slowly, in a ruined, silted riverbed. I know that mankind has wrecked my natural system, but within my spirit essence there is no judgment. When a small, frail child wades into my shallows, slipping into a deep hole, it is I that fill her lungs, unfeeling, while she drowns.

Suddenly, a strange duality begins. Not only am I the water in her lungs, but I am aware of my physical self, Michael, holding the child. I place my lips on hers and, as I begin to give her mouth-to-mouth resuscitation in a hopeless attempt to save her life, I am the water I draw forth from her lungs.

I feel the shock in my human self as I realize the little girl is an empty shell, but simultaneously with this all-embracing vision I see the mistlike form of her ethereal body as it hovers uncertainly at her side. Unable to restore her bodily life, I am aware of my humanity as I wade into the river to wash her vomit from my mouth. I am the water that swirls into my own mouth and I am the river to which I address my emotional, tear-stained words, "Please, help me to understand."

In this strange duality, where time and normality no longer exist, I reach an understanding. In some inexplicable manner, an event of twelve years ago is happening now. Some remote part of my consciousness that blames the river for the girl's drowning is laid to rest.

As mist, I float on white-capped mountain peaks, their

spires jutting through me as I hug their cold, stony slopes. It is I that transpire from the leaves of a million trillion plants, and I that return in light rains and heavy storms. Far above our planet, I perceive the Earth beneath me, and if consciousness can weep from beauty and joy, I am surely doing so.

Endlessly, timelessly, I am part of the lifeblood of Nature's system. I flow in the body of every human being, carry every life, flow from the apertures of every body, and know Oneness as a total reality.

I am water, in pond, puddle, ocean, lake . . . and river.

A huge involuntary breath brought me spluttering and gasping to my senses. I felt leaden, heavy . . . human! I was also cold, and shocked to find myself in the river. Swimming to the bank felt strangely physical. What had happened? In a flash, I remembered. I looked for Pan, glancing to where I had last seen him. Nothing! I toweled myself dry, rather disoriented. Suddenly, in clear detail, I remembered the incident involving the little girl. With a group of friends, I had been swimming in the muddy waters of the River Murray when we had heard a lot of shouting and screaming upriver. We had run to investigate and found more than a dozen people frantically searching the river looking for a little girl. The fatalistic feeling of hopelessness I had experienced washed over me with the return of the memory. The river had been so muddy that even placing your hand below water put it out of sight. The child's relatives and friends had already spent five minutes looking with frantic haste, and as we organized a more thorough search of the river the minutes ticked away. It was some fifteen minutes later that her submerged body had been found in a waist-deep hole only a few feet from the bank. One of my friends and I had worked on reviving her, but we had both known it was futile from the start.

Only now did I realize that I had never come to terms with the river and her drowning. I remember asking the river to help me understand. I realized now that the drowning had created conflict within me, for I had loved the river, muddy and silted as it was. That it had drowned the child was in no way the fault of the river; nevertheless, the innocence of the child had somehow caused me to blame the river. My journey into the essence of water had revealed this unrealized rift between myself and the river. Now, I hoped, the rift was healed.

I dressed, holding out my arms to stare at them in fascination. I knew I would never take anything physical for granted again. My arms, my body, *I* contained the consciousness of water, a consciousness separate from my own consciousness — and yet not separate at all! Somehow, Pan had taken me from my physical body and plunged me into a metaphysical realm where I had *become* water. Within that experience, I had connected not only with my past interaction with a river but with *all life,* for water is in all things. Strangely, I had not lost my awareness of myself, yet my identity had become submerged in the experience of being water. A fusion had taken place, a fusion suggesting the interconnectedness of *all* life and the possibility of our reconnecting with Nature in a way that reaches the very core of our Being. Time was revealed as an imposter in this metaphysical realm, for my encounter with the drowned child twelve years ago had been happening as I experienced it. Nature had often indicated to me that time and space are three-dimensional phenomena only, and to a certain degree I had already experienced that, but this was something else!

Three weeks passed without a sign of Pan. I moved from my initial shock into a feeling that I had been tricked. To experience the girl's drowning from the perspectives both of a human *and* of water itself was overwhelming. And yet I began to see that I was viewing life differently. I had learned that the borders and boundaries we erect and impose on life do not carry much reality. If my experience had been real—and it had felt more real than anything I had ever known—it suggested that we live within a very narrow and confined reality while a hidden vastness may await us. Who determines what is real—or not real?

Alas, although the experience was giving me a lenient attitude to the idea of life's reality, I was still having a struggle with my *personal* reality. The experience in the river had been so personal I could find no comfort in talking about it with friends. As always, I shared my thoughts with Treenie, aware of how much I needed her stability. She seemed to have no trouble accepting my account of what had happened, but I was plagued by the conflict created by my logical, left-brain self and my holistic, right-brain self. I needed to come together and function as one whole Being, but instead I was split. Both Pan's appearances and the experiences he had precipitated were outrageous denials of all that was considered normal. I discovered that normality was something I valued and that my logical self clung to it with tenacious strength.

My mental turmoil all came to a head in the most unexpected manner. Treenie and I had been invited to a party, and with some reluctance I agreed to go.

The usual hum and murmur of fused and discordant voices filled the large room. Through the crowd, I could see Treenie, looking magnificent in her dark red dress and her crown of glowing silver hair. She had gone gray at an early age, blaming life with me as the cause! Personally, I loved her hair. As the middle years had softened her face, so the silver-gray hair had accentuated it. She reminded me of a beautiful tree, which, having grown and matured, was now in full bloom. Her eyes animated and sparkling, she was caught up in conversation. Not my best at parties, I tend to flit around the periphery of the various groups, seldom making real contact. Not so with Treenie. She is a people person, a stimulating, compassionate, and intelligent woman who attracts people easily.

From my retreat behind a tall potted palm, I listened with some trepidation to the powerful assertion of a dark-haired woman as she declared her love for and need of her guru. Her eyes swept over the people around her. "We all need a guru," she stated with unshakable conviction. "We need to share in the love and wisdom of One who knows truth." I felt momentarily threatened. I had no guru, no one to direct me to that final truth. In fact, for most of my life I had scorned the notion, never having felt a need for one. Yet at that moment I found the woman's conviction unsettling and, intrigued by the power of her statement, I now met her eyes. Abruptly, I had her full attention.

"What about you, Michael?" she asked. "Do you have a guru?"

I groped for an acceptable answer and could speak only four words. "Pan is my guru."

The small group murmured. The potted palm and I became the center of attention.

The dark-haired woman stared at me challengingly. "Are you serious? Or are you in love with the eternal youth of Peter Pan?"

My words came strongly now, carrying the power of my own just-realized conviction. "I mean the Great God Pan— he of the goat's horns, hooves, and mischief by the water."

That was the end of the discussion. Nobody knew whether or not to take me seriously—and I didn't help! All I could feel was a growing sense of wonder at what I had said and now knew to be true. But why me? Obviously, I had not selected such a Being. I had been chosen. For what purpose? One thing was certain—I had finally accepted my reality. I felt my acceptance and my surrender to the will of Pan as a breath of fresh air within me.

The following morning, I made my way down the steep steps beneath the trees on the riverbank to my old bridge-plank diving board. Halfway down, I paused. Pan—naked— was standing on the end of the board! He seemed oblivious to my presence, and I watched in amazement as he leaped high into the air and came down onto the end of the board. With even more surpirse, I saw the four-inch-thick board bend and, with a supple flick, toss him into the air. He went high, far higher than possible, turning a couple of perfectly executed somersaults before entering the water without the faintest splash!

By the time I scrambled down the remaining steps, he had emerged dripping from the river. I stared at him aghast. He had no sex organs! I took two steps back and sat down on a rock. It was all too much!

He looked at me levelly, clearly amused. "Not quite what you expected."

My mouth opened and closed three times before any words came out. "But . . . but you are male, surely?"

"I am neither male nor female. I am balance. I am the infinite balance of Nature."

"But mythology depicts you as a horned goat/man who spent his time splashing by rivers and seducing maidens. How could you do that if you were sexless?"

He just smiled at me, and his beauty was overwhelming.

"If you were terrified of inhuman beauty and ran from its sight, what would you tell other people? Would you describe me as beauty or a beast? People do not like to be diminished by their own fears."

But another one of my niggling doubts had been dredged up from somewhere in my conditioned self. I stared at him, trying to see past the beauty to the beast. "Where is the traditional Pan?" I asked. "Didn't Pan cause panic? It — you — gave birth to the word *panic* and its meaning, isn't that right?"

"Not I," he said. "That was the work of man. When a person's view of life is so restricted and petty that it cannot embrace a nonhuman reality, panic is the reaction." He was again dressed in the faded green denims and T-shirt. He had not put them on; they were simply there!

Pan smiled at my consternation. "For me, this body is no more than a garment of thought."

I was bewildered. "But how could you be so heavy that you made the board bend? No matter how high I jump, it doesn't bend. Yet the other week you sat cross-legged on the water. It doesn't add up."

"That is because you believe in the fixed laws of physical reality. Believe in them. Go ahead; you need them. But do not limit your belief. Accept the fact that other realities exist. Other realities have different rules. You cannot apply one to the other."

It made sense. I did not really understand, but it made sense!

I had suspected that he read my mind. His next comment confirmed it.

"Do not be limited by what you understand. At this point, only your intellect seeks to understand. But you can allow yourself to *know directly* rather than logically deduce by means of your intellect."

I understood, I thought! But I had some unfinished business with Pan. I didn't mean to accept what he told me passively but felt the need to clear away all lingering doubts. "Why didn't you come and see me after my experience in the river? I might have drowned, for all you knew. Didn't you want to know what happened?"

He had been standing on the end of the board again,

but when he glanced back at me, fire flashed from those intense, disturbing flecks in his eyes.

"I know exactly what happened to you. I know you better than you know yourself. For a while you experienced belonging, something rare in the human condition." I was astonished. That was *precisely* what I had experienced, but until this moment I had not been able to find the word that described it. I had belonged in Nature, even though the connection was through water. I had belonged to Earth, to humanity, to life. In that state of Oneness, I had belonged in a way that as a human—and separate, as all humans are—I could never feel.

"That is where you are wrong. You retained your humanness, but the Being you are experienced the wholeness you are. You *are* all you experienced. Within humanity is the whole of Nature. Even I am part of you."

Now I was confused again. "I don't understand."

Ignoring me, Pan gave a great leap onto the end of the board, and again he somersaulted into the air . . . to vanish! I looked all around me, up in the air and into the water, but there was no sign he had ever existed. I walked to the end of the board and gazed reflectively upriver. What did he mean when he said, "Even I am part of you"? How could he be? Maybe I needed to see Pan not so much as a personality but as the Spirit of Nature. Yes, that felt right. He had already told me that humanity contained Nature, just as we were contained by it. If this were so, then Pan was part of me—and of everyone else. I smiled at the thought!

Lost in speculation, I turned to walk off the board and

was startled to see Pan sitting cross-legged on the rocks. His abrupt appearance precipitated another question. "Can other people see you? I know Kinsley did, but can other people? Could Treenie?"

"Only if I choose."

Another question occurred to me. "What happens next?" Pan had done his vanishing act again, but his words were as clear as his invisible presence.

"You'll find out!"

3
Becoming Plant

I waited and waited to find out, but Pan did not appear. He had an infuriating habit of turning up at the most unexpected times, but not when I wanted him!

During this time of waiting, I dreamed on six consecutive nights that I died. The dreams were all vivid, in full color, and different. In the first, I was in a room with several other people and knew there was going to be a nuclear explosion, though I was unconcerned. Suddenly, nothing existed. It was as if the building, room, and all occupants ceased to be. Despite this, consciousness remained: I was aware of self, even though I had no body in which to remain anchored. I felt an immense freedom. I remember thinking, "Not only is matter annihilated, but even time has ceased to exist." I felt my awareness expanding, stretching out unfettered into the universe. Then I woke up.

In each subsequent dream, I witnessed my death and saw myself buried in a clear, flowing river. Always I felt a sense of freedom and exhilaration. Never was there a trace of fear or sadness. I enjoyed the dreams, even though I felt a mite anxious about what might be involved.

The morning after the sixth dream, I went down to the river. Having been buried in a river for several nights, it seemed a logical place to seek the meaning of my dreams.

I sat on my old bridge board, the memory of Pan strong within me. It was warm and humid. Low, white clouds shielded the sun, but the heat was a warm, moist blanket. Gazing into the clear water, I remembered the incredible feeling I had experienced as the water and I had merged, becoming One. I became aware of the power of the river, not so much in its volume, for it is a small river, but in its spirit. I even felt a residual memory of belonging. I could feel the spiritual energy of river, all rivers, all water. It was to this subtle, mystical flow that I addressed my questions: What did my dreams mean? What could I learn from them?

From the silence of Nature came a response.

"Nature is the physical reality of spirit. It is not separate from the human spirit. Seeking a greater truth than the physical world reveals, you have entered this natural flow. Often—as in this moment—our coming together is on a conscious level, but usually the innate wisdom of Nature visits when the mind is asleep."

"But why? Surely it would be easier for us to be awake. We could cooperate."

"On the contrary. You resist when you are awake. You deny the existence on this planet of intelligent life other than your own. The fact that human intelligence is only a minor part of *All* eludes you. When you are asleep, your consciousness does not resist such realities."

"So what do my dreams of death mean?"

"Water is the symbol and carrier of Spirit. You have experienced this. In your dreams, water symbolized complete immersion in death. This indicates conscious commitment and dramatic change. In the six death dreams, six aspects of fear died from your consciousness. Six residues of the past died. Truly, death touched you each time."

"But how can I be touched by death and still live?"

"There are many deaths. Humanity relates only to the great death of the body. In truth, this is but one death in a series of deaths."

"How is this possible?"

"Most deaths are beyond the awareness of the conscious mind. With the development of insight, there comes an awareness of these little deaths, deaths that usually happen during sleep and dreams."

I felt pleased about all this. My dreams were obviously beneficial.

River words continued. "Each little death reveals the potential for a higher expression of the Greater Self. And that is what life is all about."

"Happy now?"

I should have been used to Pan's abrupt appearances by now, but once again I was startled. Then I became suspicious. "Who have I been talking to? You or the Spirit of River?"

He was sitting on the rocks, one bare foot dangling in the water. Ripples of disturbance ringed the area, while a huge catfish swam as close to his foot as it could get. He must have been there for ages! He looked at me lazily, while another question popped into my mind.

"Questions, forever questions. Of course I have been here all the time."

"But you were invisible."

"Not invisible. I had no body!"

By now my questions and confusion had tripled. Pan

laughed aloud, a sound not human, but of distant wind chimes.

He held up his hands, as though fending me off. "Okay, I will answer. First, I *am* the Spirit of River. We are not separate. I *am* the Spirit of Nature. Next, I am no body, so I have no body . . . unless I happen to want one." He paused, sheer gleeful fun blazing from his eyes. "Most humans spend their lives trying to be somebody. It is a joke. Everybody is really no body. You are not a body, you are a *Being* with a vehicle called a body. You are All. That is who I am. Pan means All. I am all Nature. You are all humanity *and* Nature." He smiled wickedly. "Try that on for size!"

I slumped on the rock beside him. "It doesn't fit," I groaned. "It's all too much."

"Fit or not, it's reality. You have chosen to make it fit. That's why I'm here now. Together, we have to go Beyond, and you are not yet ready. So shape up!"

"Beyond . . . !"

My memory was working overtime as I tried to recall where I had heard that before. Ah! I had it. "In the Guidestone, the Keeper of the Door said, 'If you step into the Beyond, the full force of Nature shall pivot in your Being. Misused it will destroy you.' Not only do I not understand, but I feel afraid."

Once again, I was subjected to an appraising stare from those startling eyes. I saw compassion in them—at least I hoped that's what I saw.

"Yes, it could destroy you."

"Well, then. I need help. It's easy for you to say shape up, but I'm the one who has to do it. And I don't even know what I am supposed to be doing, or how. And while I'm at it, what the hell *is* Beyond?"

He was patient, I'll give him that, even if he was infuriatingly reticent to fill me in on the details. Ignoring my questions, he stood up, leaped off the rocks as though propelled upward by a super springboard, did another of his perfect somersaults . . . and vanished.

Suddenly, my body began to shake involuntarily. I stared at my arms and legs aghast as they trembled violently. In my ears came a whisper. "A shake up will help you shape up."

"Oh, my God," I groaned. "A spirit with humor."

Gradually, the trembling grew less violent but more intense. I lay back on the bank and closed my eyes. Knowing that Pan was behind this, I anticipated his next words. Sure enough, they came. "Let go," he whispered. "It is even difficult to shake you out of that body. Let go . . . and trust."

I have no recollection at all of letting go.

Once more, everything I experience comes through perception. My visual and auditory reception increase beyond measure. I become part of the All. I *am* what I experience. For a while I float above the Earth. I am nothing— everything! I feel no anxiety, even though my humanness is with me. Very slowly, drifting like mist, I become aware of my self taking on a material form. The self that I "know" encompasses many parts of the globe. I grow over the slopes of countless hills, form thickets in myriad gullies. I am briar. As a thorny, tangled mass of vines, I grow on farms and wasteland, on roadsides and in hedgerows. I am blackberry!

For endless time, I grow and thrive. Energies I have never known are expressed through me. Beings, minute as insects, swarm over my vines, while other Beings, more vast in stature but infinitely less tangible, connect me with the Earth and the heavens. All I know is continuity. A feeling akin to human joy is with me constantly. Sounds beyond anything the human ear has ever heard connect me with all life. The human fraction of me weeps at the thought that such magnificence remains beyond normal human learning. Within this sound, no violence is possible. Strange as it may seem, I know that violence is an imposter generated by our illusions of separation. All connects. Sound, minute and greater Beings, blackberries, Earth, the universe . . . and Beyond.

Seasons pass. I experience the bursting energies of spring, when the activity of minute Beings on my vines, within my form, and among my roots, is at its peak. I am the swelling buds along the stems of every briar. I am the force of life that reaches deep into the warming moisture of the soil, and I am the vines that respond. I am the leaves that slowly emerge. I am the sap coursing along endless veins of countless plants. All plants are One plant. There is no separation. Neither space nor distance exists beyond the physical form. Compared to my totality of energy, my physical form is infinitely small, yet of vast importance.

As the heat of summer grows stronger, I am the chemical changes that take place within the physical plants, and I know that without the minute and greater Beings, this could not be possible. I am the fruit that covers the vine, its flavor, its juice and substance. And I thrive.

Eventually, disturbance becomes part of my energy. My formless, invisible body is hurting. A distortion is taking place within my etheric structure, and all life is affected. I cannot become separate. I cannot shield the All from this discord. Discord enters harmony and a nonstate comes into being. I am the pain of discord, the joy of harmony. In ways that are indescribable, I suffer.

I search for ways to alleviate this discord. Helped by the Beings of Nature, I search for the source of pain . . . and I find it. Humans!

On a farm in the mountain foothills of Tasmania, a farmer sprays his blackberry vines. On thousands of other farms, on countless roadsides, blackberries are being sprayed. My discord becomes part of the discord of Nature as powerful chemical sprays are released on the plant kingdom all over the planet. And this discord connects with all life. The sprayer and the sprayed, all are equally affected. As blackberry, I am immediately affected; as a man, I am indirectly affected. The greater the delay, the greater and more devastating the effect.

I am both farmer and blackberries on that hillside in Tasmania. My awareness of being a farmer is total as I concentrate on poisoning and killing the cursed blackberries. I want the land they sprawl over, forever spreading and encroaching on my farm; it is land I need. Equally, I am blackberries being sprayed. In the vast silence of Nature, I call out repeatedly to that farmer to cease the folly of his actions . . . and we remain separate. As the Spirit of Nature, I see the incredible dichotomy of reality. We are connected, totally One, yet the farmer's sense of separation fragments our Oneness. Oneness does not cease to be. It cannot. But it remains beyond the farmer's experience of life. Outside his reality, it is unreal! Seasons pass, and each summer the chemical sprays become more toxic, more abundant.

Each summer I call into the Silence to that one particular farmer. In my knowingness, I see the time bomb within his consciousness, for his consciousness and mine are One. It is primed and due to explode. I throw my energies into activating that explosion, knowing that it will forever change his life. Within, the etheric realm's other Beings of Nature clamor into his dreams, his subconscious.

One day, the moment comes!

He/I am once again spraying the chemicals of distortion onto his/my vine body. I call again into the silence, and he responds. He yawns mightily and turns off the engine of the tractor, deactivating the pump. In the sunshine, on that warm, mellow hillside, he responds by going to sleep, an unusual act for so busy a person.

He dreams. He dreams that he is blackberry vine, and he experiences the distortion of the chemical effect. He learns that killing a physical vine is of little consequence, especially if it is done by natural means, but that his spray is wreaking havoc in the etheric regions. He experiences that havoc, and in his dream he groans aloud. I am the dream and the dreamer. I am the cause and effect. Within all this, I can sense a rightness, a movement within Nature

51

that I know can precipitate balance. I know that the time bomb in consciousness is primed in many human Beings, and each in his or her own way will trigger his or her personal explosion. When the farmer self wakes up, he stares at the blackberries in awe. In consciousness, he, human, connects with me, vine. He climbs to his feet, rolls up the long hose, and climbs onto the tractor. He starts the engine and drives away. He never sprays chemicals on blackberries again.

My blackberry consciousness covers the planet with no more difficulty than my conscious awareness of my human body. Where blackberries exist, there am I. I know that changing the actions of one human is of little physical consequence, but nothing is an accident. In consciousness, this one human connects with all humans, and this one human has long, long ago chosen to go Beyond. I know that this is a pivot point. His life, all life, has been irrevocably changed.

A sharp, stabbing pain lanced down my neck. I groaned. Where was I? I sat up, gazing out over the river. The memory of my experience was suddenly so powerful that I sat still as a statue for long minutes. Wow! What an incredible thing! I had been blackberry! Who would have thought such a thing possible? The feeling of going beyond biological limitations clung to me, invoking wonder. For a moment, I questioned why it had been blackberry of all possible plants, but then I knew. This was yet another aspect in

Nature wherein I had created disturbance and imbalance. Not only was this within myself, but within Nature as a whole. It seemed that my journeys into Nature were designed to give me an opportunity to redress the imbalance while simultaneously learning and expanding in awareness of self. How I could be shaken from my body I did not understand, but I realized with an ever-deepening insight that our bodies are indeed no more than wondrous vehicles. Essentially, we are not the reflections in the mirror!

When I arrived at the house, I looked at the clock. No more than an hour and a half had elapsed since I left! I called Treenie and over a cup of coffee told her all that had happened. I recalled how I had once, many years ago in Tasmania, felt a strange, overpowering impulse to sleep when I was spraying blackberries. The dream had changed me, I recalled. After dozing off on that sunny afternoon, I had dreamed I was spraying blackberries. Not unusual, considering! While I sprayed the deadly toxic mist over the leaves of a particularly vigorous blackberry, I had heard a voice calling me. I stopped spraying and looked around, but there was no one there. The voice called again, telling me to touch the leaves of the blackberry vine I had been spraying. I did so. As my fingers touched the leaves I was hurled into the air at tremendous speed, up and up, until I was far above the Earth. Looking down, I could see the whole of our planet, and for some peculiar reason all the blackberry vines were clearly identifiable and visible. I saw, to my astonishment, that from this elevated view they formed a wholeness, like one whole plant, yet I knew that they were really many individual vines. As I saw and real-

ized all this, I began to fall to Earth, feeling very frightened. Suddenly, my fall was checked, and I began to feel
a terrible despair. I cannot describe that feeling, but it was
awful. I felt as though something was dreadfully wrong,
so wrong that it would cause the downfall of all life as I
knew it. This was not a physical feeling, not even a mental one. Rather, my whole psyche seemed to be in torment.

I began to fall once more, and as I fell I felt that all
Nature was crying. Then I saw myself, as though on a
screen, spraying the blackberries—and I knew with utter
despair that I myself was the cause of that profoundly
disturbing feeling. Then I woke up. The dream had been
too strong or clear to ignore, and I never again sprayed
blackberries or any other plant with toxic chemicals.

Together, Treenie and I speculated on a strange possibility: the blackberry experience had occurred *then* even
though it appeared to happen now. In some incredible way,
my dream of all those years earlier had been interwoven
with the *present!*

I say that we speculated, but in truth it was I who speculated. Treenie listened patiently while I rambled on, trying to convince myself that time was as malleable as
memory itself.

Then Treenie spoke. "My darling," she began. When she
begins like that, I know I am in for a lecture, sometimes
a patronizing one! She continued. "If there is one thing
we have learned along our path, it's that time, space, and
separation are all illusions—powerful ones, perhaps, but
illusions all the same. When you have a mystical experience
that verifies truth, why do you fight it? Why is it so difficult

for you to accept what you already know? You know in your heart what is true. If I can understand it, I know you can. You have been exploring the consciousness of the plant kingdom. It was a metaphysical experience, because you can't put a physical body through such antics." She smiled at me sweetly.

"There's no need for sarcasm," I muttered.

"Oh, but there is. You persist in deliberate and pointless nonacceptance. Assuming that you can be more reasonable and open, let's sum up the situation. Your experience revealed to you that all life is connected. You learned that whatever we inflict on Nature will eventually be inflicted on us. Yes?"

"Yes. And *by* us!"

"That's the irony of it. As long as people see Nature as being outside themselves, we will continue in such folly. Responsibility for the planet begins with each of us. Little did you think when you were spraying the blackberries that you were causing all Nature to suffer. Your mystical experience reveals that individual action has a universal application."

Her eyes sparkled with enthusiasm as she continued. "I find it exciting that what you learn on a metaphysical level always seems to have a physical application."

"That's because they are not separate. Each contains the other. Gee, aren't we limited," I concluded as I realized how little of what we were discussing was involved in common knowledge or thinking.

"Don't get morbid," Treenie admonished. "That's your problem. Part of you doubts your metaphysical self and gets morbid. You even doubt Pan. You see him, yet you doubt him. Do you doubt me? Just accept that when you are learning a new game, you have to learn different rules."

Then came the nice part. She put her arms around my neck, kissed me, and said, "I'll help you, my darling. That's why I am here."

That part always bothers me. She often tells me she is here to help me. She also says I came here under protest. Now *that* I can believe!

A few days later, down at the river, I decided to try and conjure up Pan my way. "PAAAAAAAAANN," I shouted, as loudly as I could.

"You called?"

Pan was standing only a few feet away. It was all too much! It made me wonder how often I had been unaware of his presence.

"More often than not," Pan stated.

I sighed. I knew it was true.

He gazed at me, locking my eyes. I could neither blink nor look away. He looked pleased. "It's happening," he said. "Experiencing Nature as it *is* takes you farther and faster than listening to disembodied words."

I felt slightly devalued.

"Why do you do that?" Pan asked. "In no way do I belittle listening to the silence of Nature. The words of Nature have immense value. I *am* those words. But they are not the experience." He frowned at me. "Sometimes I wonder about you."

I scowled back. "It would help if you would answer a few of my questions. Just the important ones. Like what *is* Beyond? Why do I have to go there? What have I been chosen for . . . and why? Those will do for starters."

Pan laughed a human laugh, long and loud. His eyes were a challenge to me. To be unable to look away from someone's eyes can be a chilling experience. Sometimes he looked right through me. How many times had I read that expression in a novel? But actually to experience it was something else! The flecks of light in his eyes contracted and expanded as though animated by an independent life of their own. I had the feeling that I was seeing the universe shining through those flecks of light. It was as though I was seeing beyond . . . Beyond!

"Aha! Now we're getting there." Pan's voice was mocking. "*Life* is Beyond. Life, in all its many facets. Other realities await. You have been chosen because long, long ago — that is, if we concede to subjective time — you made the choice to manifest in this earthly dimension. You chose to become a sleeper — and you chose to awaken. The process in which you are now involved is the awakening. It is a planetary process. Each individual on this planet is part of the whole, or, to put it another way, the whole in a part. As each individual awakens, every other individual is affected, for, as I have said, the whole and the individual are One." He smiled strangely. "There is a catch, however. Awakening does not simply happen. You have to want it. You have to become aware that humanity is asleep. You have to become aware that the events of daily life are a dream, a collective dream that most of humanity shares and unwittingly believes. So, you must choose to be different. You must choose to let go of restrictive and limiting beliefs.

You must choose to create thoughts that lift you beyond the mire of negative human thoughts. You must choose to become creative with your own Being. You must *choose* to become awake. Becoming awake is to know who you are—to know your Greater Self. Humanity is struggling to awaken—or at least some of its members are. Some choose not to."

"Why do they choose that? You would have to be mad to choose to stay asleep."

"They make the choice by not choosing. They dream not knowing they sleep. The same problem afflicts the whole planet. Some tune into the new energies, some tune them out. That is their choice. Those who ridicule and scorn what they do not understand, what is unknown because it is *new,* will cling to the old."

"So what have I been chosen for? Correction: what have I chosen to do, and why?"

He chuckled, light flashing from his eyes.

"You have chosen to help the human consciousness awaken. You are but one among many. As a writer and speaker, you have adopted the perfect tools. And to you have been drawn those who long ago elected to help humanity awaken. You have *very* enlightened help."

A long-held suspicion came to the surface. "Treenie is part of that help, isn't she? I used to think she was a fallen angel. Without her, I would still be asleep."

"You are not yet awake, but you are in process and, yes, Treenie has chosen to help you. As for her being a fallen angel"—he looked thoughtful, hesitant—"she has not fallen."

4
Becoming Mineral

I had not seen Pan for nearly a month. Despite this, I tried to continue my relationship with Nature. I could connect with and listen to that inner voice of silence, but it was no longer as satisfying. Pan provided another dimension of Being. When I was with Pan, a keen throb of anticipation beat within me, for I never knew when the miraculous would unfold around me.

Treenie and I left home quite early one sunny morning to visit one of my favorite places, a great flat-topped pillar of rock towering high above surrounding forest in the New England National Park, only a couple of hours' drive from our sheltered valley.

We walked the track through dense, dripping rain forest until we reached the base of the plateau. From there, we followed the steep track to the summit. Below us, as far as the eye could see, lay forest. On the ridges it was sparse, open sclerophyll—dry, stiff-leafed—forest, while on the plunging slopes grew rain forest, lush and soft, reaching deep into the valleys. Each environment was clearly defined; together they appeared from above as a patchwork quilt of varied shades of green.

My eyes lingered on the gray rock face at our feet. It was jagged and crumbling, stark testimony to the erosive power of the wind, rain, and ice. Bird song, spires of thin, rich melody, ascended from the trees below. For once, I had a bird's-eye view onto gently swaying leaves. On this small, bleak, windswept plateau high above the surrounding forest grew hundreds of bonsai. Small and ancient sprawling shrubs clung with tenacious roots that had penetrated deep into ancient cracks and fissures. How different were the forest giants, so close in distance yet environmentally so far away. They have had little struggle in their efforts to grow. I wonder . . . where lies the greater strength?

"Penny for them!"

I glanced at Treenie, startled. It was so easy to get lost in the sheer grandeur of Nature in a place like this.

"I know you're planning to sit out here and attune with the plateau," she continued, "so I'm going to find somewhere sheltered where I can absorb the view." She gave my hand a quick squeeze and wandered away. The soft, eerie moan of the wind as it swept over the plateau had intensified, and clouds now filled the sky.

I sat on a low, uncomfortable shelf of rock buffeted by the unceasing wind. In front of me, a strange phenomenon unfolded. Pan slowly emerged from . . . nowhere! He appeared as a phantom, without substance. Hesitatingly, I reached out to touch him, and my fingers passed through his misty form. I felt very uncomfortable with this arrangement. His smile had no clear definition; even his eyes were vague, distant. "I wish you were a bit more solid. You seem too much like a ghost for comfort." My words were an intrusion.

"But you are the same!"

Startled, I hold out my arms. Sure enough, they are no longer flesh and blood. I drop them onto my lap. I feel normal to my own touch but am as nebulous as Pan. Only then do I realize that we are slowly sinking through the solid rock. I look at Pan for reassurance.

"You have experienced the consciousness of water and of plant, all the while 'knowing' your humanness. Now you shall experience crystal, and you will 'know' your human connection within the kingdom of minerals. Deep within your psyche is hidden knowledge. You must connect with this." Questions surge in my mind, but the strange experience I am involved in is too immediate to be denied.

The sensation of sinking through rock becomes more pronounced. We seem to sink for a long time, yet the time is unmeasured. Around us, rock flows past with no more substance than a heavy gray cloud. At the end of the descent, I find that we are enclosed in a huge cavern, still seated on the shelf of rock. The darkness enclosing us is pierced and vaguely illuminated by countless flickering points of light. I get to my feet and glide across to the nearest wall of the cavern. Studded and dotted in the rock walls are millions of tiny jewels, flashing and sparkling with great intensity. Although the light they produce remains constant, the jewels shine in an ever-shifting iridescent pattern. The sight is breathtaking.

I brush my fingertips over many of the jewels, curious. Some are cold, some hot, but most are cool. None are loose; not one lies casually on the rock floor. Above me, around me, at my feet, each one is firmly embedded in the rock. But where is Pan?

I listen to my own thoughts speaking to me, yet they are not *my* thoughts. Suddenly, I realize that this is telepathy! Inside my head, I hear Pan.

"There is a reason for you to be here. Find it."

Perplexed, I saunter around the cavern. It is very different from the huge chamber in the Guidestone. Movement is easy here. Even as I decide on a direction, I am moving along it. I examine the walls some more but can find no new or startling revelation.

"What sort of reason?"

I am ignored. This is a place of no-time. One part of me seems to wander around for ages, but in a greater sense time ends. Gradually, as I absorb the feel of the place, I gain the impression that I am seeing merely the tips of one huge crystal. Each separate jewel seems to be a single facet of one, while the bulk is hidden, shielded by impregnable rock.

"Good. Your perception is correct."

I can hear him, but I cannot see him. And I want to!

"Do you think you could become visible? This place is beginning to give me the creeps."

"I am here. Do not be afraid. Take notice of the flickering points of light. Can you imagine the One light? Each human being has the potential of the One, for each is the All. There is no separation between you humans, but what do you do? You each bury your individual light in negated thoughts, ignorance, complacency, and apathy, and through the ages these maladies have become solid as rock."

I feel acutely uncomfortable.

"And you are now firmly embedded. Only sparks emerge, glints of your submerged potential."

There is silence.

Then blazing, awesome, overwhelming light.

"*This* is the potential of being human."

Even as the words reach my mind, I am picked up by some vast, inexplicable force and hurled out into—nothing!

I seem to be floating on my back, at ease. I can identify nothing around me, but I appear to be enclosed in a huge cocoon of light. I am at peace. Nothing disturbs me. I stay in this suspended state for a period of no-time. Gradually, I feel a very faint sense of urgency. It is tugging at me, drawing me from my undisturbed peace. I resent this, for the peace is beyond anything I have experienced. The urgency persists and unwillingly I sit up. It is a strange feeling, for I am suspended, floating, yet my body is without substance. At the far end of the cocoon, the light is dispersing and I can see through it. Before me appears a scene from three years ago, but as I watch, it is happening *now*. Irresistibly, I am drawn toward the end of the cocoon and precipitated into the unfolding scene.

"I've got something to show you." Linda Tellington Jones was excited as she hurried into her room. She was staying with Treenie and me for a few days during one of her regular visits from America. When she reappeared, she showed us a bluish green crystal about the size of a woman's fist. It was rather opaque, lacking the clarity of a Yang crystal or even the milkiness of the Yin. Peer at it as I might, I couldn't see within it.

"This is an aquamarine," she said fondly.

I wasn't at all a crystal person, but I felt duty bound to "oooh" and "aaah" over it, while Treenie appreciated its beauty in a more genuine way. Linda, in a typical display of enthusiasm, declared her intention to have it sliced in half. "One half for you, and the other half for me," she said, beaming at us.

Treenie looked dubious. "I wouldn't have it cut if it were mine," she said, concerned for the crystal and for Linda.

"I think it's a great idea," I said, concerned for neither.

Only a few hours later, we were at the Quartz Crystal Awareness Centre, where Ian MacArthur also considered the proposal with caution. "It may spoil it," he said. "It could be sliced easily enough, but we'd have to find the right place." He turned the crystal over and over, until he reached a decision. "Yes, it could be cut here." With his finger, he drew an imaginary line, inviting our comment.

"Be careful," said Treenie.

"Cut it, cut it," Linda cried excitedly.

"Are you sure it will be okay? We don't want to ruin it," I said, but in the next breath I urged him to cut it.

With some apprehension, Mac took the crystal into his workroom and sliced it into two halves.

It's important to explain that we are talking about a very valuable gemstone. Mac had never even seen one of its size and quality. The deed was done and, though Linda was unrepentant, I felt slightly guilty. Mac showed us the revealed interior under a strong light.

Wow! It was a crystal transformed. I could see myriad tiny spires of light stretching from the outer surface into the marine depths at the center. Light caught and held the needle spires, coating their lengths in rainbow colors. I was hooked by the beauty and mystery of the rock's interior.

Not long after Linda returned to the States, I laid our half of the aquamarine on my desk and opened up a conversation with it—at least I tried! But no matter how I focused on that elusive energy, nothing came to me from it, not a single whisper.

A year passed, and the crystal remained mute. But one day while I was gazing into the aquamarine's window, watching the play of light on those tiny threads of inner space, it entered my mind to take the gemstone to the ocean and place it in a rock pool. So, one sunny morning in midwinter, I took the stone to a particular rocky headland where there was a group of large rock pools. The tide was right. Everything was perfect.

As I walked along the beach carrying the crystal, a small group of rocks caught my eye. In the hollow center of one rock was a small pool, containing no more than a bucketful of water. When I had walked a hundred yards farther along the beach, clearly into my mind came the words, "That is my pool!"

"Aha!" I muttered. "Mute no more!"

I trudged back across the white, crystalline sand to the little pool and placed the aquamarine in the water. When I had settled myself on an adjoining rock, a feeling of well-being came over me, and I knew its source was the gemstone shimmering in the pool. Within moments, an incoming wave sent a sheet of clean ocean water into the little rock pool. I gazed at the crystal, which was caught in a shaft of diluted sunlight. A thousand rainbows formed and vanished in its interior.

"Do you hear me now?"

"Oh, yes," I replied. "Very clearly."

"Long have I known your consciousness, but to intrude was . . . untimely!"

"But why? I have wanted to hear you. I can appreciate that you must be an incredible storehouse of knowledge culled from vast spans of time."

"This I acknowledge, yet you still need to release your hostility to crystal energy. This is strong within you."

I thought about that and decided it was not true. "No," I protested. "Not hostile, just indifferent."

"You think so. Look into the depths of the crystal and see what you see."

I gazed down at the crystal. Swirling water and sand flecked its surface, and it looked rather mundane. But as I lifted my eyes and glanced out over the ocean, another seeing emerged, an inner seeing into another reality.

I see myself, even though I am in an unfamiliar body, inhumanly tall and lean and in a very different landscape. It is early morning, well before the rising of the sun. The era, I sense, is long past, compared with the time I call our own. I stand alone in a small valley, an amazing valley! The mountains around me are crystal; sheer brilliant spires emerge from a white, solid base. No human eyes have ever seen the like. This is a place of dreams, a place both alien and hauntingly familiar.

I know that I am about to die, yet this is my choice, a choice made in the name of science. I am conducting an experiment, an attempt to transfer my psyche beyond my body. To what destination? I do not know. I cannot reach deeply enough into this other me to learn it.

I am aware that my loved ones are watching from a shielded place within the crystal mountains, and I am aware, too, of my own immense sadness, combined with a will and a desire to live. The act I am undertaking is not a casual one. It is the result of long and detailed studies. Many experiments have been carried out, but this is the ultimate moment. Only now may I know, and only I can be subjected to this devastating, one-way experiment. I am very old, having lived far, far beyond a human life span, and am filled with a boundless, inhuman knowledge. I have no fear whatsoever. I experience curiosity, regret, and, strangely, exultation.

As I stand in the valley, a huge alien sun rises above the crystal mountain as though part of a smooth, clockwork motion. The sun is much larger, much closer, than our own. Light reflects back and forth along the blazing spires in shafts of great intensity. Despite the double lids on my eyes, I am instantly blinded. I am unable to see the sunlight when its awesome energy is focused on one huge central crystal spire, and I feel nothing as the light blazes through me. As though hit by a colossal fist of wind, I am hurled inward, then outward, then into . . . nothing!

I am back in the safe, serene comfort of the cocoon of light. I am floating on my back, at peace, yet the memory of all that has taken place is with me. There is no anxiety. Everything that has happened fits into a sequence of my life that in this state of suspension feels perfectly natural. I am aware of being nourished, of being protected from immediate shock while I assimilate the events that have unfolded. There is a period of no-time. I know that I am the human me *and* that other, alien self! In my memory, the blazing light of the exposed crystal and the terrible blinding light of the alien sun mix and merge. There is no separation. No time has elapsed. Both are happening . . . now! I am shocked and exhilarated. I know both my selves, even though the alien self is unavailable. I cannot tap my alien knowledge or look at my alien thoughts. I have learned that time is not a constant factor but part of the human construct. The voice that whispers as a distant echo in my head is comfortingly familiar.

"So much of human roots are in the endless past, yet not the past of the time span most humans live within. Reality is flexible, timeless, limitless, unbordered, but the human concept of reality is strictly limited. For your species, it is conditioned and bordered by your belief in separation. This isolates each one of you. The past you briefly experienced in the crystal valley was you of another reality, a reality that in its past coexists with your present."

"But why, Pan? Why? And what happened to that alien me?"

"What happened to that distant you connects with you *now*, but the experiment and its results are not this moment's conjecture. You will experience that experiment again, and at that time you will be ripe to enter and experience just what did happen. You are not ready yet."

"Where was I, Pan? *Who* was I?"

The whisper becomes very faint. "Questions, always questions. Question not who you were but who you *are*, for in the journey you have undertaken, this is the paramount question. If you lose your self, how are you to find it again if you do not know who you are?" His words are fading, and in direct proportion the cocoon of light is also gradually fading away. The irrational thought that I might fall from this state of suspension crosses my mind, and a shout gathers in my chest.

My voice, loud and startling, made me jump as I shouted into the wind.

I was still sitting on the shelf of rock on the plateau in the bonsai forest, my heart hammering away like a sledgehammer. I took a few deep, steadying breaths. I no longer enjoyed the protection of the cocoon of light, and my mind was a spinning chaos of images from the multiple time frames. I tried to slow my mind and put it all in careful order.

The experience had begun exactly where I was sitting. First, there had been the sensation of sinking down through the solid rock with Pan; then we had emerged into the huge crystal. There Pan had shown me that all the many flickering points of light were *one* light. As I experienced this, Pan had shown me the vast power of that one light—and I had literally been blown away! My next awareness was of being suspended in a cocoon of light, safe and protected. Where this cocoon was I had no idea, but I suspect it was somewhere between dimensions, in a place of no-time. After an indeterminate time in this cocoon, I had seen myself of three years ago involved in a clearly remembered incident with the aquamarine. Next thing I knew, I was out of the cocoon and into that past, but living it as though it were now! I had taken the aquamarine to the beach and placed it in a rock pool. The aquamarine had told me I was hostile to crystal energy. After a short interaction, I had had an incredible vision—of myself as another type of Being on another planet standing within a crystal valley. I had been conducting some sort of experiment in psyche transference. The sun had risen, and a shaft of light of unbelievable power and intensity had totally disintegrated the body of that other me. The experiment had been successful, for the psyche had survived and had been hurled out into other dimensions and realities. I paused in my thoughts.

It was only now that I realized this, yet I *knew* it to be true. Immediately after experiencing the blast of light from the sun, I was back in the cocoon of light. For a while—I have no idea how long—I was nurtured. I needed to be cared for in that way! Then, faintly, I heard Pan's telepathic words. As his voice faded away, I had felt that I might fall. My shout had brought me back to an earthly, three-dimensional reality where time ticked away to the beat of a watch on my wrist.

As though to prove that I was back, Treenie came to where I was sitting on the rock ledge. "You've been sitting here for nearly an hour and a half. It's time you had your lunch. I've had mine." Then, seeing my face, she asked, "What happened?"

I looked at her helplessly. "I think I've put it together in my head, but I really can't talk about it yet. I feel numb."

She nodded sympathetically. "Are you all right?" she asked anxiously.

I nodded. "I'm okay. I'll have my lunch up here. Then I'll come. There's plenty of time." I smiled at my unintended pun. Treenie pointed to the clouds. "Don't get wet."

I watched her as she walked away, aware of the feeling of warmth and love that connected us. Within that love, I knew, flowed the endless thread that connects all life.

I ate my lunch sitting on the sheer edge of the plateau, overlooking the forest. A strong wind buffeted me, whipping my hair with playful indifference, and I began to feel refreshed and more clearheaded. The images no longer jostled each other in my mind, but the feeling of numbness continued. It was not a physical thing, but rather as though something was smothering and dampening the intensity of my feelings.

My reverie ended abruptly when a few drops of rain, driven by a fierce wind, stung my face. Treenie was right. Time to go!

I followed the track across the plateau and down the tumbled, jumbled pile of huge rocks to the forest floor. In this calm and sheltered place, the rain was negligible, and as I followed the track homewards I tried to quiet my mind by concentrating on the natural abundance around me.

Away from the track, the dense forest was almost impenetrable. This was a place of rare and startling beauty, where a thousand different species of plants competed for the diffused sunlight that filtered through the leafy tops of restless trees. And what trees! Host to an incredible variety of vivid mosses, lacy ferns, gray and yellow lichens, and strange liverworts, the tree trunks were almost buried in clinging vegetation. My thoughts returned to my experience on the platcau, and I wondered where Pan had gone—and when.

"It is not I who withdraw from you. It is you who become unaware of me." Pan's words seemed to echo around me, but I could see nothing of him.

"Where are you?"

"I am within the forest. Everywhere you look, I am." I shrugged, not ready for more lessons. His voice, when it came again, was strong and stable, but he was still invisible.

"Relate to me as though I am all the trees around you. You do not need my form right now."

There was a long pause. "Michael . . . give me a summary of your experience. Not what happened to you, but what it meant to you. Tell me what you learned and what you feel."

I felt vexed! "You know what I think and feel. What's the point?"

"Yes, I do. And I can also feel the numbness and shock you are experiencing now that you are back in the physical realm. I want to hear you express your feelings and thoughts verbally. I want you to hear yourself."

I knew he was proposing therapy. It did seem appropriate and he was certainly the right person—person?—to listen to me. To my surprise, my words came tumbling out. "I learned that the human view of reality is little short of pathetic. Our normal reality is like each of us living in a tiny, windowless cell in a house that contains a hundred thousand rooms and covers a thousand acres of land. We believe that the cell is all there is, so we live in it isolated and alone. What is even sadder is that if a few people like me manage to tunnel out of their cells and see some of the other rooms awaiting entry, the majority of people think we are imagining things." I paused for a moment. "Not only do I think that, I also feel it."

Pan's voice was a soothing caress. "You seem hurt."

"Yes. Somewhat to my surprise, I am."

"Why?"

"Because in some way the strangeness of my experience separates me from other people—not in reality, but in knowledge and experience."

"That's easily rectified."

In a flash of clarity, I understood. I could write a book about my experiences, just as I had written the earlier book about talking with Nature. It had taken a measure of courage to write that book and expose my soul, but this one would be much harder. Still, I knew I could share my experiences with honesty and clarity. The rest was up to the individual reader. Knowing this, I felt better.

"Anything else?"

"Yes. I learned I was hostile to crystal energy. I suspect that the experience with the alien me was to show me why. Also, I'm aware that there is a lot of unfinished business regarding that other me, but I feel comfortable with that. Everything has its timing." I grinned. "You taught me that. I understand what the heart of the plateau crystal had to teach me. It told of our need to learn that humanity *really* is one family. We really *are* all brothers and sisters. In fact, in consciousness we are even closer. I learned that time and space form only a three-dimensional reality, and that it is possible to allow the psyche to expand and journey into other realities, other times. I also learned that I have a lot to learn!"

I waited for Pan to respond, but only the whispering of countless leaves answered me.

I continued on down the track toward the waiting car— and Treenie.

5
Becoming Animal

Treenie and I had been idling away the morning, chatting over a few cups of coffee before she left for a few hours. For some unknown reason, I felt apprehensive as I watched the car accelerating up the road. Dismissing the feeling, I returned to our sitting room.

Ever able to surprise me, Pan was sitting cross-legged on the carpet in the middle of the room. His curious eyes held me in an appraising and serious gaze.

"Sit down and relax."

His words were not an invitation; they were a command. I sat down.

"Make sure you are comfortable."

I swallowed nervously. "What's going on?"

"Relax."

It made me more tense to hear Pan tell me to relax in such a serious tone. "I knew it. Something nasty is going to happen, isn't it?"

Pan smiled and, almost against my will, my anxieties dissolved. I resented his easy control over me, but my reasoning part quickly became unreachable.

"That's better. I look serious, I know, but there is no cause for alarm."

I took a deep breath. "I've been apprehensive for the last hour. I don't know what you have planned for me, but I bet it's the cause of this feeling."

He smiled that irresistible smile—sunshine breaking through clouds that had lain heavy for weeks.

"It is time for you to make another connection. The Door to Beyond beckons. In your quest for self-realization, you must connect with the kingdom of animals. Humans are not animals, even though you classify yourselves as such. Humans are a different form of Being. Humanity contains the consciousness of animals, just as you still contain the consciousness of the vegetable and mineral kingdoms. You, Michael, have connected with the consciousness of the plant and mineral kingdoms and with water in its many forms as it covers and penetrates this world."

I was pensive. "I seem to be involved in a process of experiencing Oneness—to actualize and become *one with* Nature, going beyond words and ideas." The connection of words suddenly became apparent. "Is that what going Beyond is? Is it going beyond all words and ideas? Is it in fact going beyond the limitations of the mind?" I felt excited.

Pan's eyes flashed approval. "As near as it can be verbalized, that is what going Beyond means. However, Beyond *is* a reality. It encompasses this time frame and more. Now, let's get started."

I felt apprehensive. "Wait . . . wait a minute." One of Pan's pencil-thin eyebrows arched inquiringly.

"Do I get to choose which animal I experience?"

"Oh, yes. That is absolutely essential."

Thoughts of cheetahs and other of my favorite animals crossed my mind. Then a terrible thought popped in, uninvited. "I won't be killed or eaten, will I?"

"Is that in your experience of animals?"

I thought about it, a bit uncertain. "No. Not that I know of." I had a terrible feeling that something was being over-looked, but what?

"Then *go*."

There was no gentle shaking, no easing out of the body. His words were a vibrant force within me, hurling me out into . . . nothing!

I am a cattle dog, a puppy. Everything is a mystery to be gnawed on and played with. I understand little. I live in the eternal moment, and within that I have fun. I have a companion my own age, and all day we play, sleep, eat, and play some more. We fight mock battles, and in our play we grow stronger and more coordinated.

There are other cattle dogs on the farm, two mature grown dogs who regard us with amused tolerance. To-gether, my friend and I grow beyond puppyhood, becom-ing aware of a strange craving within us.

One day, our master comes to us and puts us in a big vehicle. He takes us on a long, bumpy, smelly journey. It excites me. I have never smelled such smells; the wind is full of them. In my excitement, I lose control of my blad-der, but my master only laughs. When we stop, he takes us out. We are restrained by a chain attached to our col-lars. He talks for a while to another man and then departs without us. I am devastated.

Next morning, the other man feeds us, takes us to a large, airy barn, and introduces us to some other puppies and grown dogs. Each day he takes us out into the fields, and with shouted instructions and help from the adult dogs, he teaches us how to round up and drive cattle. They are stupid creatures, nowhere near as clever as I, but there is a lot to learn. I find out the hard way that a single cow and calf are not the same as a herd. I approach a cow and her calf, and she charges me. I am surprised when one of her horns catches me. Luckily, I am only bruised. It is a good lesson.

Time comes and goes, but for me there is only the joy of working with cattle. I no longer have the strange craving. I am totally satisfied by my work. The man is very pleased with me. He pats me often, calling me a smart dog. One day, my master comes to take me home again. My companion does not come back with us. He stays on the farm and is contented. He does not love my master in the way I do. He would accept anybody.

I am now a large, strong cattle dog. Master has names for us. I am called Spud, and my eyes are odd colored. I have white eyes, and my master tells me how unusual this is. The other dogs are Ringo and Bounce. I like them. One day when master shouts the familiar instructions to us, Bounce does not come home. We all run to get around the cattle, but Bounce keeps going. We never see him again.

Master has a lot of cattle, and as the years pass I want nothing more than to work them. Often there are strange urges in my body, and I dream of desirable female dogs. Sometimes these dreams are so strong that when I wake up I run around restlessly looking for the female, but the lack of scent tells me I have only been dreaming. Once, a female does visit the farm, riding on the back of an open vehicle. Her odors are very exciting, and I want to couple with her, but I cannot get off the chain, even though I struggle. I am very upset by this and take my anger out on Ringo. I am bigger and stronger than he is now. We have a fight, and I am top dog.

Several years pass, and then something devastating happens. Our master no longer milks cows in the dairy near my kennel, and we have no work to do. The master takes us out into a paddock, securing our chains to a long wire pegged down at ground level. We have plenty of space to exercise but seldom any cows to work.

And something else happens. The master has been changing over the years. I can see it in his energy. I can read his intent as easily as I can read a cow. It radiates from him. He has been linking his consciousness with his beef cattle. Now, when he wants them moved, instead of using Ringo and me, he communicates into their consciousness, and they leave the paddock where they are and go wherever he wants them to go. I am very upset.

As dog, I begin to experience frustration. A growing, gnawing emptiness fills me, and I become angry. I growl and snarl at Ringo, for he is the only available outlet for my anger. He becomes the focus for my frustration and rage. As the months pass, instead of easing, my anger becomes worse. Ringo accepts the situation with the cattle, but I cannot. I become more morose, more vicious.

Our long wire runs are too far apart for us to tangle chains but near enough for us to drink from the same water bowl and touch noses. One day, when I am feeling particularly angry, I hurl myself against the chain—and it breaks. Ringo barks at me, telling me not to be foolish, and in red rage I attack him. I can feel a blinding red heat behind my eyes, and I am filled with the urge to tear and render. How it happens I do not know, but I kill him.

When it is over, I slink into my kennel. As the heat and rage leave me, I know I have behaved very badly.

Once more, I am duality. As a human, I approach the odd, distorted body of Ringo. In the pit of my stomach, I feel despair. Kneeling down, I hold his stiffening body in my arms. His stomach has been ripped open, his vital organs bitten to pulp. I look at Spud, knowing the inevitable. I chain him up, holding his head in my hands. I am not angry, but sadness is a heavy weight as I realize what I must do. With four young children, I cannot risk keeping a jealous dog. I assume that Spud has killed Ringo from jealousy, for I know how attached he is to me.

I watch my master walk away. I know he is going to kill me. I have seen him shoot other animals. The energy around his body is heavy, filled with sadness. I live only in the moment, so I do not fret. There is only now, and right now I live.

When he comes back, he is carrying a gun. He is very upset. I wag my tail furiously. I am not afraid, even though I know my death is here. I need to work cattle, not live on a chain. I want to run free, chasing on the heels of huge herds of cattle. A dull thud smashes my head to the ground, an explosion of light, and I am up and running, free as the wind. In countless other cattle dogs, I feel my consciousness working and fulfilled. I am Ringo. I am Bounce. I am Spud. I am All in One, One in All. I am dog, all dogs.

I am crying as I aim between Spud's strange white eyes and squeeze the trigger. He drops soundlessly, boneless. Falling to my knees, I hold his head in my hands, my body shaking with sobs. Guilt coils and writhes within me. Regrets for things that could have been overwhelm me. I bury Spud with a heavy heart. My feelings of having acted to protect my children are inadequate, and I feel a failure.

I am consciousness, floating in the ethers of our planetary system. I am assimilating the experience of being dog and man as One. As a dog owner, I have failed, and my guilt is a pain. I know now that I shot Spud for the wrong reason. As the psyche of Spud, I know he would never have harmed any of my children. He had not been jealous. He was born to work, and work was denied him. I know that he holds no anger toward me. He is free, united with all dogs. I am that unity also. But I am human, and I find it difficult to forgive myself! Nowhere in my dog reality is there blame or anger, only love. As dog, I become aware of the burden of guilt that humans carry, and I try to love it away.

Gradually, awareness withdraws from separate aspects of the dual psyche, and I become myself sitting in a chair in my sitting room.

I lowered my head and cried, all the suppressed pain erupting in a torrent of tears when the deeply hidden guilt finally came to the surface, as in a long-festering wound.

And I felt rage. How dare Pan trick me like that! He had known I was going to experience something awful. Why hadn't he told me what to expect? Why hadn't he even hinted that I should be prepared. Without doubt, he had known what awaited me. I cried for a long time, tears coming to the surface from some deep source. When I noticed that Pan was back in the room looking at me, I ignored the compassion and love in his eyes.

"You tricked me!" I spoke with controlled vehemence.

"Michael, I love you. Why would I trick you? It was you who determined where in the Nature of animals you would go. You, yourself, connected with your unfinished business. What is unresolved in the past remains unresolved in the present."

"Why didn't you at least warn me? That was a horrendous experience! I suffered from both my human and dog aspects. I loved and died, and killed both dogs—one I tore to death, the other I shot. Do you wonder I feel betrayed? How could you let that happen to me?"

Despite my anger, I knew he had been right—I *had* made the choice. I had felt misgivings when he told me I would choose my own experience. His next words were very unwelcome.

"I am sorry, but it is not yet ended. You had the opportunity to let go of all your guilt feelings concerning your connection with animals, but those feelings continue to fester within you. If I *had* warned you of what to expect, you would have *expected* the experience and therefore rendered it totally valueless. As it is, you can now see the emotional chaos you have been suppressing regarding your role as a dog owner. You must deal with those feelings or there can be no further progress."

Fists clenched, I felt my anger flare. "That suits me fine. I've had enough of this anyway. I got shot out there. I felt it in my consciousness. I got killed. I died—even though I'm not dead."

"And do you remember the feelings within your animal consciousness toward your human self? Do you remember the love that dog felt for you? You were the dog that loved and you were the human with guilt. Why do you cling to the guilt and deny the love? Why are love and peace more difficult to embrace than pain and discord?"

I knew I had become irrational, but I could not stop myself. All I wanted to do was lash out and hurt. "It's easy for you to talk. It wasn't you out there being shot or feeling guilty as hell. I seem to suffer no matter which side I'm on." Lost in anger and confused emotions, I jumped to my feet and stalked out of the room, dismissing Pan.

A month passed by and I saw nothing of Pan. Once I had recovered, I realized how silly I had been. He was right. He always was! I told Treenie the whole story. I shared with her all that had happened during my experience as the consciousness of dog and of my angry reaction to Pan immediately afterwards. With her help, I explored my feelings. I knew the experience had not ended. Somewhere out there—in there?—I had to connect with an essence of myself, or of life, that I did not yet comprehend. I had to deal with my guilt. Pan had made this clear and I realized that until I resolved my guilt feelings I could make no further progress in my quest for self-realization. How strange that my relationship with a dog should be the stumbling block. With all my human lives and my multitude of experiences, I had no feelings of guilt that I was aware of. I may well have lied, cheated, slain others in battle, and maybe even committed murder in my various incarnations on Earth, but I felt no guilt. Maybe I had worked it all out, leaving the slate clean. I hoped so! But with the animal connection, I carried this guilt.

With Treenie listening sympathetically, I recounted some of my memories of Spud. During our decade as farmers in Tasmania, cattle dogs had been essential to the easy and efficient movement of the cattle. Spud had been outstanding as a working dog. In keeping with the farmers' tradition, I had not allowed the working dogs to become household pets, but nevertheless I had become very attached to them.

I sighed at the thought of all the changes I would have made had I experienced dog consciousness then. Both Ringo and Spud had excelled in their skills. I could send them to the farthest paddocks, a mile away, to bring the cows home. I used to boast that the only thing they could not do was open and close the gates!

The problem began after we finished milking. At this stage, I no longer needed the dogs to work. To make matters worse, I had been practicing communicating with our cattle by "thinking" them to where I wanted them to go, all in accordance with the inner consciousness of the cattle. This effort had been so successful it had made the cattle dogs practically redundant, so I stopped using them and put them on long running chains so they could get plenty of exercise.

"Should I have sold them?" I asked Treenie.

"What do *you* think?" she parried.

"It wouldn't have made any difference." Even as I spoke, I knew my answer was true. The guilt had merely been brought to the surface by my experience of shooting Spud. Somewhere in my past lay other painful encounters.

The sharing and exploration of my feelings helped me understand that I still had work to do, but I continued to feel frustrated about my reactions to Pan.

"Be patient, my darling," suggested Treenie. "Pan won't desert you. Allow yourself to remember the actual experience of being dog. Write it down. Maybe you will learn something that Pan is waiting for you to learn."

I recaptured in memory the love I had felt as Spud. Even death had made no difference. Going through the transition from physical, individual dog to dog spirit had been without trauma. As dog, I had not clung to the act or the moment of dying. I had remained dog, loving and generous.

Only in my human self had pettiness been present and, worst of all, I had directed it at Pan . . . and myself! Perhaps I needed to learn to treat myself with greater love and respect!

I was concerned that I had driven Pan away forever. "What should I do?" I asked Treenie. We were having breakfast and the thought of another day without Pan was disturbing.

"Why don't you apologize to him?"

I stared at her in indignation. "If I could do that, I wouldn't have the problem, would I?"

Treenie is ever patient. "You have told me that Pan is in all Nature. He is in the trees and in the river. Why don't you go down to your favorite place by the river and simply apologize aloud."

"That's a brilliant idea." I smiled in approval, then I frowned. A question that had often niggled me came to the surface of my mind. "Do you resent me having this relationship with Pan? Do you ever feel jealous . . . or threatened?"

Treenie gave me a level look of appraisal. "At the beginning of it all, I thought I might," she said candidly, "but not anymore. I'm your physical and spiritual partner. We are soul mates. So why should I feel threatened by a Being who shares only your metaphysical life? That he is for your ultimate good and inner growth, I don't doubt. I can't resent that. Besides, you spent years attuning with Nature on the farm and then a few more years of more concentrated attunement down by the river. If Nature responds by revealing that there is a mystic dimension to all that only appears physical, and a teacher comes from that other dimension, should I object? It seems to me that you have earned the right to encounter a Being like Pan."

I kissed her!

Later that morning, I went down to the river. Standing on the end of the diving board, I called out. "I don't know if you can hear me Pan, but I apologize. I was overemotional and rude. I'm sorry. I want you back in my life. I miss you."

Two strong hands held me briefly around the middle— and then pushed. I hit the water with the sound of wind chimes ringing in my ears. Surprise! They continued chiming while I swam underwater! I came up laughing.

Together, we sat on the old bridge board. I gazed at his faery beauty with deep appreciation, while his golden eyes regarded me with amusement and affection.

"Nothing has changed, you realize." There was concern in his voice.

"I'll do what I have to do. I guess it's a case of either trust you or quit. And I know I couldn't quit!"

"You have to go back into the experiences of your own connections with animals. It may be rough, but there is no other way. Your path to Beyond requires that you journey into the consciousness of Nature. You must experience Nature's metaphysical perspective and accept it. You must learn to let go of emotional attachments, becoming as free and unencumbered as the breeze." He laughed. "That's all!"

I swallowed in apprehension. "As you probably know, I had another really bad episode with a dog. I had to shoot my much loved Great Dane, Whisky. She was ailing with a cancer. I chose to shoot her rather than call in a vet. Now I wish I hadn't." My eyes misted over at the memory. "When I recall her life, there are so many things I could have done better."

This time, I could see the compassion in Pan's eyes.

"Don't you feel in retrospect that you could have done many things better? Relating to people, for example?"

"Oh yes, I do, but I don't feel guilty about that."

"Why?"

I sat for a while thinking it over. "I think it's because I view people as being responsible for themselves and for their own actions, but domestic animals are the responsibilities of their owner, as is their behavior."

I felt comfortable realizing this, and for a while there was silence as we watched the river sweep past with soft, hesitant gurgles.

"Pan. Do I have to experience the Whisky trauma?"

His voice was level, calming. "Only you can decide. If it is resolved within you, then it is finished; if not. . . . "

"If not, then I'll find it all happening again." I winced at the thought. "And there's nothing I can do to prevent it. What a prospect."

I felt shaky. "Will you be with me when I journey out?"

"Yes, but as Spirit. I cannot help you. I cannot change anything. You are totally responsible. You determine whether you will suffer or not. You are the experience."

"I wonder that you still have patience with me. I have failed in my reconnection with Spud, and I know I'll fail if I relive Whisky's life."

"What nonsense you talk. Failure and success are illusions. As long as you measure yourself in terms of success or failure, you will remain unenlightened."

I thought about that, trying to find a way to rephrase my words. "Well, I didn't succeed with Spud, did I?"

He laughed. "Nor did you fail!"

"Didn't I?"

"You experienced an inner connection. You made a connection with the consciousness of dog, and your emotions were too deeply involved for you to perceive with clarity and insight. You are too harsh on yourself. Acknowledge your capacity and merits. How many people do you think could make such reconnections and come out unscathed?"

That was a line of speculation I had never considered.

"Only you judge yourself," he went on. Nothing else in life does this except humans. Humans judge themselves and each other. Give it up. You don't need it. Judgment is an unnecessary burden. Did Spud judge you and find you guilty, or was it you who made that judgment? Believe me, Nature makes no judgments."

I knew Spud hadn't. That had been particularly obvious.

Pan moved over to the bank, and I followed. I sat down beside him.

"Are you ready?"

"Oh! No!"

"Good."

For an eternity I encircle the planet. It all seems familiar, a planet I have visited many times. Slowly, without any sense of time, my consciousness becomes more solid, taking on form. In many, many separate bodies, I roam the Earth, but gradually my focus becomes one single animal. I am a dog. I experience my self as separate, yet my awareness of connecting with the All is ever present. There is only Now. Thoughts of soon or late are nonexistent. Within the Now, beyond any need of thought, I am connected.

I am a large dog, a Great Dane, and I live on a farm in the foothills of Mount Arthur in Tasmania.

I experience my years of puppyhood by eternally playing with the children who live on the farm. I live in the house with the family, spending the winter evenings on a rug before a blazing fire. I am loved, and that love is part of my connection with life. I need love; I thrive on it. To be stroked and patted is rapture. The vibration of my owners' Being is transmitted by touch. Their love is as vital to my well-being as food.

When I am full grown, something dreadful happens. I am dismissed from the house! I no longer sleep on the rug before the fire. I feel that I am shamed, but no punishment for misdeed is inflicted. Nobody tells me why I am banned from the house and garden, but it happens.

I am given a new bed in the soft hay in the hay barn. I lack nothing in comfort, and if the evenings are more chilly it does not greatly concern me. What festers within me is the lack of stroking and touching on which I thrive. But I cannot reflect on such matters. I live what is. If something is missing, it is missing for all time.

I grow older, less capable, while the children of the farm become stronger and more capable. My special attention is always focused on the master of the farm. A look of love from him lights me up; a frown of anger devastates me. That he loves me is apparent. I can read his energy as easily as I can read any human energy. Humans are an open book. Emotions play out in streams of energy around them, signaling their intentions long before they act. Sometimes, visitors to the farm are deeply repulsive to me, but this is rare. Many fear me because of my size, but fear is their constant companion; I only externalize it. This I know, because in the Now their energy broadcasts their feelings to all Nature. Humans cause me fear and pain, love and joy. A fearful human *is* fear, transmitting the emotion to me and the other dogs. We snarl in rage, hating the vibration, and the fear grows stronger.

Love is my life. To love and be loved is my purpose, and I know this with every atom of my Being.

The disquiet I feel at being removed from the house is never in my head, but it is *me*. I become that energy. The ruling never has to be enforced. Once removed, I know the rule but never why. I am never tied up. I have freedom. The whole farm is mine to roam, but the house and garden are banned.

As I grow older, an ache develops in one of my front legs. Gradually, it becomes a deep-seated pain, not intense but an endless throbbing. I limp, and this is difficult on my long, rather clumsy legs.

I ail, moving less and less frequently from my snug bed in the hay barn. I see less of the children, and this also becomes a pain. I see far less of my master as well, for his work consumes his time. Only when he feeds me do we physically connect. I deteriorate rapidly in health and condition. One day, my master comes to me, and I know he carries my death. The distress emanating from him is terrible, and my fear for him is paramount.

Suddenly, there is duality. I am dog, suffering from a growth in my leg, and I am master, crying as I hide my gun behind me.

He wraps his arms around my neck, and I feel him shaking in anguish. And I am my master, as, wrapping my arms around Whisky, I cry with what I have to do.

I watch, unresisting, as he levels the gun at me. I know it kills, for I have seen it in action. I know he is going to kill me, but I have no fear. I have no knowledge of death. I am dog. I live, I love, I bark, I die. None of these are separate.

I am the man, shaking with contained grief as I take aim between the eyes of the trusting dog. I see those limpid eyes of devotion gazing into mine, and I can hardly hold steady. Taking a deep breath, I squeeze the trigger.

I gaze into those blue human eyes, and my love pours forth. Abruptly, there is a tremendous shock to my head followed by a far distant explosion. I am no longer in pain, no longer contained by an ungainly body. I am light, free, spirit of dog, loving my human master. I gaze at him as he holds the bloodied head of my dead body. I try to lick the tears from his face. I want him to know that I bear no grudge, but he is unaware of me. I want him to know that I love him, that death is only a movement in life, one I have experienced many, many times. But all he feels is grief . . . and something else.

I hold the shattered head of Whisky and let the grief pour out of me. My thoughts hold only one phrase: if only, if only! If only I had let her live her life in the house with us. Why did I allow such petty issues to change things? So she knocked the children over with her great size. So what? Did they ever complain? So she left a large pool of saliva on the lounge floor where she slept! How trivial it now seems. I cry, cradling her head in my arms, her blood mingling with my tears. And I feel the guilt of my failure. As a dog owner, I have failed, and my guilt is a pain.

The consciousness of dog self and human self merge. As human, I become aware of being Whisky and all I can feel is an overwhelming love for my human self. I become aware of having experienced this connection to resolve all the guilt that has accumulated in my human psyche. I try so hard to let it go . . . and I open my eyes, staring tearfully up at the sky.

The words of Pan come to me as soon as I open my eyes, soothing, yet powerful. "Let it go, Michael. Focus on the love of Whisky and the love of Spud. That love is *now*, Michael, not some time in the past. Focus on love . . . and *go*."

I am hurled out of my physical body with immense energy. The soundless blast of power, though enormous, is totally painless. I spin over and over, my mind empty. Space fills my consciousness forever and nothing exists. No form holds me, no physical entity attracts me, and for eternity I am nothing. I am Beingness.

Gradually, with incredible slowness, my consciousness focuses. I run, swift as the wind, over the Earth. I am pure nervous energy in physical form, but I live in exhilaration! I am hare. No, not *a* hare, but *all* hares. When danger threatens, instinct draws forth the required behavior. I become immobile, perfectly camouflaged and blending into the Earth. Or I run, racing over the soil with abundant vitality.

Nothing exists but Now. I live, mate, fight—and die—without a care or worry. Life is exuberance, an endless overflowing cycle of dynamic tension. I fight with other buck hares, experience the breathtaking delight of mating with the does, and as a doe I watch in keen pleasure as other bucks fight for the right to mate with me.

In a cycle of seasons, the fields on which I live are sown by the farmers; they change from bare earth to green oceans of food and then to golden corn. Here I live, safe and secure on a thousand farms. I live also in meadows and wild land, untamed by man, but my focus becomes a number of hares on a particular farm in England. Each year, huge machines devour the yellow corn in which we live, and each year comes the terror.

I am a young man, riding the combine harvester as it circles the field of ripe, golden wheat again and again. I am excited, for the field is full of hares. Each time I circle the field, it becomes smaller. Now, hares are beginning to rush out, ears laid back as they run for their lives. I pick up the shotgun and with easy familiarity swing it snugly into my shoulder. I fire, and a hare pitches head over heels, screaming its pain and agony. I fire again and again as the hares run the gauntlet for their freedom. I am proud of my ability to shoot.

I am hares, ears back, running in terror from the approaching monster. I comprehend nothing. All is fear . . . and running. I have no knowledge of what to expect. I run.

In a dozen hares, I run like the wind, and pain and oblivion smash into me. Yet I run, leaving behind the struggling forms as they kick out their abundant nervous energy. I am long gone, no longer physically limited as I race across the Earth. I am free. I run from shattered bodies and have no knowledge of death. It has no reality. As *all* hares, I am on the physical Earth, but I also roam the ethers and their etheric structures. There is no difference, no separation.

I am human, I am hare. Our consciousness mixes and merges. I know that as a human I carry the consciousness of all hares within me. Nature and humanity express the same consciousness of One. We are linked, irrevocably. I feel no guilt at my actions as a young man. I knew no better. Hare is hare and I was me.

I am consciousness, a thread connecting all living creatures on Earth. I am briar. I am rock, alive and vital. I am cloud, drifting on the high winds of consciousness. I am cattle dog, living on a farm in Tasmania, and I am Great Dane, loving my master. I am hare, running fleet of foot. I am bird, singing on a branch in a garden. Winter is ended, spring is here, and I sing with the joy of life.

I am a small boy, creeping down to the garden with a brand-new slug gun. I am excited, a great hunter. I see a robin, high in the branches of a tree. I stalk the bird, oblivious to the beauty of its song. Quivering with excitement, I raise the gun to take my first shot at a living creature. I pull the trigger.

In the middle of my song, I am struck in the throat. I fall to the ground, but even before my physical being has landed, I am free, flying to a tree of shimmering light to finish my song of joy. My joy is even greater now, for here there is no fear. I am *all* robins. I am *all* song.

I pick up the tiny carcass. I feel ashamed. A single drop of blood hangs trembling on the red feathers of the bird's breast and now I remember the beauty of the song. Tears flow from my eyes. I wish desperately that I could change the bird back and hear it singing again from a bursting heart, but I know this is impossible. I bury the robin and erect a tiny gravestone in a secret place. For twenty years, it is a constant reminder never to shoot another robin. I never do.

I am consciousness, connecting all life. I am aware of self and of my connection with Nature. For endless time I move in and out of various animals and birds. I experience a lizard, but it is a time of dull instinct, connecting once more with my childhood.

I am cattle. I am many cattle on the foothills of Mount Arthur. I am aware of a changing relationship between us and the farmer who cares for us. After a time of total separation, we begin to connect. We begin to trust him. We feel his growing love.

I am a single cow. I am sick. As the farmer feeds us hay one winter's day, he notices my distress. He walks me out of the paddock, away from the other cattle, and down the hill. We are on the familiar walk to the cattleyards, but my time has ended. I know this, but the farmer does not. Within me, the new life I carried has ended. I do not know why. At the bottom of the hill, we cross a creek. I turn off the road, and, following instinct, go into the creek. I stand in the icy water and the farmer tries to make me leave it.

I will not. I am ready to die. A natural process is taking place. I feel it and trust it. To leave my body is to return to the One. I want this to happen. I am sick. I am in pain.

I am seething with frustration as I try to get the cow out of the creek. She is a cow I have reared on the bucket, and I am very fond of her. I know that she has a dead calf inside her, and I fear she has peritonitis. Everything I do to get her from the creek fails, and after two hours I am exhausted. Finally, as a last resort, I put a halter over her head, and tying the rope end to the Land Rover, I drag her bodily to a small tree. There, I tie her securely to a branch, before driving up to the house to phone for the vet and to change my soaking clothes.

I go back to the cow. She is a big, well-bred, strong cow, overdue to have her second calf. When I get to her, I find she has broken the branch off the tree and is back in the creek. She is lying down, and the icy water is flowing over her body. I am very distressed. I realize that the water will numb any pain in her body, but I know she is going to die. So many times I have seen cows die. Often, when a cow knows she is going to die, she will arch her head round her back into a classic dying position.

I sit down helplessly. The cow looks at me, making deliberate eye contact. She holds my gaze. I am surprised. Animals rarely hold eye contact with a human. Even a dog will look away after a few moments. She stares into my eyes and I read her knowledge of her own death. There is no fear within her. I am crying. I am bonded to my cows and I do not want this to happen. Into my head comes a thought, a knowing. She does not recognize death as an ending; it is continuation. She has no emotion regarding death, but I am all emotion. I must learn to see life uncluttered, rather than through the clutter of intellect. Misused, emotion and intellect are handicaps. They distort my view of Nature. The knowing ends, and through tear-filled eyes I watch her head arch around her back. Then, calmly, without fear, she places her head underwater and quietly drowns.

I am cow. I stand beside my drowned body in the creek. I am connected with the consciousness of all cattle, but something strange is happening. Something I recognize as a Higher Being is beside me, filling me with a knowing beyond cattle knowing. I had waited with this Being for the farmer to come and witness my death. He understands so little as he weeps out his emotion.

As he quiets, I connect with him. I am able to do this because he has learned to link with our consciousness. His eyes open wide in surprise and, through me, the Higher Being pours forth a golden energy. I see it clearly, shimmering as though a cloud of dust surrounds the farmer. He sits down, his head in his hands. But only for a moment.

Something peculiar is happening. I am sitting beside the dead cow, but I am no longer human. I am consciousness. I am connected with all Nature, all Life. I see beyond the deceit of death, and I know life to be the totality of what *is*. I know that I am responsible only for myself and that Self connects with All life.

As briefly as a blink, it is finished. I am sitting by the dead cow. My sadness remains, but deep in my psyche there resides a greater knowing. Somehow, sometime, I will connect with that Greater Self.

I am consciousness. I am joy. As a human, I have recon-
nected with my own inner knowing. Now I know that I
know! I spin through the etheric structures of reality and
experience a hundred other animals. I become cat, renew-
ing the many times we have come together, and I find immense satisfaction within this union. I become wallaby,
playing out the trauma of my years shooting these gentle
creatures, and I no longer hold onto guilt and judgment.
I allow life to come and go in its endless cycles, no longer
deceived by the physical illusions of form. I become an
eagle, closely bonded with human self as an Indian in North
America, and I am falcon in old England. I become a
jackdaw linked with my childhood, and the union is bit-
tersweet. I become magpie and man in a recent encounter,
and I have the knowing of bird. Every creature I become
is a connection in my life as a human Being. Some of the
connections in consciousness last for years, some are a brief
moment, but in all-time there is only no-time. An eon, a
second—there is no difference.

Tumbling, drifting, no-thing, every-thing, I am back in
my human body.

Another reality. I was stiff; I ached! The riverbank had
not been kind to me and the small stone under my neck
had become a boulder. I groaned, physically exhausted,
but inside me there was joy. The breakthrough had come
with the death of the cow. Memory took me back to those
farming years when her physical death had taken place.

She had looked at me with her huge, brown, expressive eyes, and in some way I felt a knowing. Insight had surged within me, revealing my emotional state at the time. Crazy as it had seemed, I had *felt* that some other presence was with us, but as I had stared anxiously around I could see nothing. I remember one logical part of my mind trying to rationalize the feeling by thinking that it could be the vet, yet I also knew that was not possible.

I stood up and stretched, easing away the kinks as I thought about all that had taken place. Going back into my death as a cow and experiencing it from a metaphysical perspective, I had *seen* that other Being. Should I be surprised that it was Pan? All those years ago, Pan had given me an insight that, by defying subjective time, had now assisted me in my battle to go beyond my emotional relationship with animals. Pan had given me a brief but penetrating insight into the totality of life. I had seen that life as one continuum, not a series of beginnings and endings, and, even though at that time I had not been able to take that leap of understanding, the view had helped me.

The joy of my recent triumph was a warm inner glow. Having experienced the dying cow and my emotional self on a spiritual plane, I had somehow experienced a fusion within my consciousness. My emotion had become revealed as if it had been a thick fog obscuring the view of a great valley. That my emotions were still my own was apparent, for tears trickled down my cheeks. But my feelings would no longer cloud my perception of the animal consciousness or block my ability to reach a greater insight. With the emotional attachment ended, I had been able to flow into a whole series of other incidents involving other animals. Each had been without trauma. The experience of shooting wallabies — and of being the shot wallabies — had flowed without hitch. I had laid aside blame and judgment, allowing the continuity of life's expression to be revealed. It was a good feeling!

I walked up the steep steps slowly. Now I had made one more step in my overall journey into a holistic Nature. I had connected with plant, mineral, *and* animal consciousness, resolving all the discord that had inadvertently accrued between myself and Nature. I was aware that this was my particular path, but we each walk the path of our choosing, and I knew that I was not alone in consciousness. We are *one* humanity.

6
Within a Storm

The day had been unpleasantly hot and humid, and we speculated eagerly about when the inevitable thunderstorm would strike. During the afternoon, ominous black clouds had gathered and, although I looked forward to the cool relief of the impending storm, I felt an odd apprehension.

"I don't like the look of this at all," Treenie stated, as she joined me on the lawn. Together, we stared up at the clouds. A slight breeze pulled gently at our hair and stirred the leaves on the trees.

"Neither do I. I reckon we're going to have one hell of a storm. I'll go and make sure the henhouse is secure and check anything else I can think of."

For the next hour or so, I was busy. I laid heavy planks on the henhouse roof, braced the garden shed, and generally prepared for a violent night.

The storm was slow to gather, but this gradual building only heightened my anxiety and increased my apprehension. Throughout the afternoon and into the evening, the storm slowly gathered power and momentum until the valley was filled with clouds. These seemed different from normal storm clouds. It was as though an inky pigmentation had leaked from some malevolent dimension, staining the clouds with impossible layers of darkness. These clouds met and merged with night, bringing the day to a premature close.

We ate our evening meal in a subdued silence. Even our teenage children were quiet, affected by some outside influence. The racket of television was a welcome distraction, and our choice for comedy was unanimous.

Not until eleven o'clock that night did the storm begin, commencing with a torrential downpour. Anticipating a disturbed night, we straggled off to bed, but sleep was impossible. Around one o'clock in the morning, with the darkness seared and illuminated by almost continuous lightning, the whole household was awake. For quite a while we stood on the verandah, watching in subdued awe, literally overwhelmed by the sheer physical enormity of the storm raging over the valley.

As our family members retreated bleary-eyed back to their beds one by one, my persistent inner anxiety became even more intense. Continual deafening blasts of thunder combined with vivid, twisting flashes of lightning and a powerful gale-force wind that failed to move the storm away. It all induced a deep-seated unease. Staring spellbound into the storm, I became aware of the similarity between this and the forces inside the Guidestone. Yet there were differences. In both cases, power was involved, but the power seemed of two kinds and of different orders.

I am a light sleeper, so I decided to sit in the living room for a while. Our electricity had failed, but in the flickering candlelight I could see our two Abyssinian cats cowering under chairs. Half-heartedly, I tried to evict them, but they resisted strenuously. Owing to the cats' habit of bringing rats, mice, snakes, and other undesirable prey indoors to devour, these two were always shut out at night. This

indignity—even during most storms—they had long ago
accepted, but not *this* night! With a shrug, I allowed the
cats to stay. I blew out the candles and sat back in an easy
chair to watch Nature's grand display of fireworks.

For maybe half an hour I watched light flicker and flash
around the room. Rain drummed on the tin roof in a heavy
roar, while the thunderous sounds of violently released
energy raged overhead. My heart thumped with inner tension as I tried unsuccessfully to relax.

Suddenly, during a startling crash of thunder, I saw that
Pan was in the room.

His appearance was so completely unexpected, I was
shocked. "What are *you* doing here?"

Pan seemed larger and more powerful than I had ever
seen him. The energy emanating from him was almost as
electric as the storm itself, and suddenly I was chilled with
worry. His words rang inside my skull, while he stood back,
looking remote and alien.

"The Door to Beyond is not easily entered. So far, you
have experienced the inner realms of water, plant, mineral,
and animal consciousness. This is the Nature you are comfortable and familiar with. I have told you many times that
humanity is of Nature, not separate in consciousness.
When humans misuse Nature, the environmental impact
soon reveals the effect of that abuse. Equally, if humans
physically or mentally abuse each other, the negative
effects are quickly revealed in your everyday lives and rela-
tionships." He paused, his impassive face turning toward
me, his eyes holding mine. I swallowed nervously, unsure
of what was coming next.

He continued. "More subtle by far, yet no less power-ful, is the effect of negative thinking in the natural world. Nature is affected by negative action *and* negative thoughts. Seldom do humans realize this. Very rarely do humans even consider the possibility that the quality of their thoughts might affect Nature. You have experienced the results of your own negative action in spraying toxic poison onto blackberries. Now you have the opportunity to experience the cumulative effect of negative thinking. You will ex-perience the effect this can have in Nature."

Thunder pealed and crashed around us, but Pan's words were crystal clear—too clear!—in my head.

"But why?"

"Because you are a part of that negativity. With *very* few exceptions, all humanity is involved. If you agree to ex-perience this dimension of negative human power, you will benefit. Because you are not separate in consciousness from other people, they will also benefit, even though they will be unaware of it."

"*If* I agree? You have never given me a choice before!"

Pan shook his head slowly. "You made the choice to journey into the hidden realms of Nature. Thus, each ex-perience and its content has been your choice. You know this. This time, however, you can refuse the experience."

"Why?"

"Your previous encounters have involved your own per-sonal relationship with Nature. This one involves the wider human relationship with Nature. You are only a part of that."

"You've told me I can refuse. But can you tell me what to expect if I agree?"

"No. You will have to go on trust."

"On trust of what?"

"My love for you."

On a reckless impulse, I blurted out, "Okay, I'll do it."

Immediately, Pan dramatically increased in size. This Pan, one I had never seen before, loomed huge, fully fifteen to twenty feet tall. In some inexplicable manner, he stood right up into the roof of the house, and it was as though no house or room existed. His size was horribly intimidating, yet there was no menace in the hand that reached out to me.

Unthinking, I took it.

With appalling strength and power, I was snatched out of my body and hurled like a rag doll up, up into the violence of the storm.

I am lost. Although formless, I am battered and exhausted. For long ages I am tossed and torn within the raging forces and seething energies of incomprehensible turbulence. I sense conflict of a type totally unknown to me, something that surely dwells in dimensions of madness. All around me, an awful blackness tries to engulf shattered, scattered fragments of rainbow-colored light, while pure whiteness of incredible intensity writhes as though in pain among patches of malignant gloom. In some way, I seem to be protected from the maelstrom of violence that engulfs me.

I watch, feel, as segments of whiteness seek to combine

and fuse with the rainbow-colored light yet are hindered by the black turbulence. I am helpless. I have no power to assist, although my whole Being cries out for the light. I struggle, feeling like a tiny child held tight in the arms of a giant. For ages I strive ineffectually to help, but I have no form, no way of reaching out. I am exhausted.

Gradually, into my consciousness comes an idea. Within the grayness of my Being, a tiny spark of hope slowly grows into a small, twinkling light. Eventually, responding to this inner light, I do the only thing I can—I visualize the rainbow-colored light and whiteness as One.

The result is catastrophic, for in that instant my protection is gone. Instantly, as no more than a tiny mote of human psyche, I feel the violence and raging fury of the maelstrom enter me. I am shattered, fragmented, torn into a million fragments of rainbow-colored light—but in that moment, a new awareness literally explodes into my psyche.

This storm, of vast and awesome proportions, is of humanity. I recognize it as a manifestation of our collective fear, born from our rapacious greed and appalling negativity. *This* is what Pan meant. The rainbow-colored light is symbolic of our highest human ideals, while the terrible blackness is our own negativity. It hampers our collective endeavor in our struggle to reach the light—pure Love. It is our negativity that hinders our spiritual evolution.

I am torn to pieces, hurtling around in the center of the storm as though I were a million grains of sand in an endless cyclone. But I hold onto my knowing and a faint determination slowly grows stronger, gaining strength from my insight into truth. As my own determination grows, I feel that within my psyche I make a connection with the rainbow-colored light.

Instantly, a rainbow forms, whole, new, invincible, and I know that the human potential has no limits. My determination is no more than a mere echo of all human determination.

Regarding me with stunning indifference, a Being beyond anything in my experience reaches out to embrace me within its formless energy. Its words, which I hear as soundless, crash as thunder into the physical world.

"Just as the suppressed rage of an individual eventually explodes in temper, so also the accumulated fears, spites, and hates of humanity unleash all the forces of a tempest."

I can hear thunder pealing with the words, but I am held in the soundless vise of an unbreakable grip. The words continue, echoing in my consciousness.

"Human beings have the collective potential to create a fine song of harmony in the atmosphere, but instead you create the heavy storms of discord. So divorced are you from your true reality that you do not recognize your negative manifestations. Many of the storms of destruction that rage above you are the reflected storms that rage within the human psyche. As within, so without. A storm of Nature compares with the negativity of humanity in the manner of a snowflake with a drop of acid."

For a long moment, there is nothing. All time, violence, and storm have ended. I hang suspended, contained in a furious hush more frightening than the maelstrom.

Then, into the shocking silence, come the final words.

"Only by surrendering to the storm is it possible for you to conquer it."

This said, the power I sense grows to proportions that are indefinable. I feel that the whole universe is involved, but in a detached manner, like a child prodding a reluctant ant with a big stick. I feel that *I* am the reluctant ant, being toyed with by powers and forces so far beyond my human comprehension that even to probe with thought is no more than trite insanity.

In a manner I do not understand, I am able to allow self to yield, neither to resist nor invoke. I realize that to surrender is to cease my struggle. By becoming resistless and defenseless I become vulnerable, and I know that I will find peace here in the same way I found peace within the turmoil of our community. Within the collective human consciousness, there is peace as well as negativity, and it is to this peace that I surrender.

Slowly but surely, the peace within me grows stronger. The rainbow is luminosity itself. In this sphere of peace, the storm begins to abate, and I know with a surge of joy that we humans can overcome our negativity.

Abruptly from the roily space, a single, brilliant shaft of lightning blasts from the black clouds to Earth, and my total awareness is centered in a rigid body in a chair. It is my body, that which I call me!

I was totally wrung out! I had to concentrate on relaxing, limb by rigid limb, as I eased the aching, muscle-locking tension from my trembling body. During this time, as I tried to come to terms with what had just taken place, the storm abated, gradually losing its fury.

It was now nearly three o'clock in the morning. Climbing stiffly to my feet, I stumbled into the bedroom and fell exhausted into bed. My last fading thought was never to trust Pan again!

I slept late next morning. By the time I got up for breakfast, Treenie was having a midmorning cup of tea. "Whatever time did you get to bed?" she asked.

I regarded her wearily. Despite a long shower, I felt jaded. "About three o'clock."

"And what were you doing so late?"

"You wouldn't believe me if I told you."

"Oh. Why should I stop believing you now?"

"Okay, point taken. Pour us both another cuppa; we're going to be here for quite a while." So saying, I launched into the story. Details were etched clearly into my mind, so I took my time. When I had finished, Treenie gave me a strange look of admiration. "You really are something, you know? You really are."

I felt pleased. But I had to be honest. "Don't forget it was that deceitful cosmic clown who did it to me. He tricked me. 'Trust me,' he said, and then he hurled me into the heart of a terrifying storm. If I had had the slightest intimation of what I was getting into, I would have run from the room."

"Which is, of course, why he didn't tell you."

"Maybe so, but that was the last metaphysical experience I want. I came out of it shell-shocked! He literally threw me into it." I scowled at the memory. "Never again! I'm finished with trusting him."

The more I thought about it, the more indignant I became. Treenie got up and made us another cup of tea. For a while she clattered around, and I knew that she had things on her mind.

Sipping on her fresh cup, she began to share her perceptions of my experience. Finally she asked, "Do you think if Pan had politely asked you to enter the heart of a storm you would have considered it? Come to that, would you have thought it possible? What choice did he have?"

"Just whose side are you on? I'm fed up with Pan. He's too cold-hearted."

"You're avoiding the question."

I squirmed.

"I'm waiting. Face up to it and confess. Pan had no choice. I have to lead you by the nose to everything you achieve in life, while you kick and struggle all the way. Look at our journey around Australia. You would have settled for something safe and secure a dozen times if I had agreed. Same with Homeland. If you could have wriggled out of that initially, you would have." She snorted in disgust. "Pan asked you to trust in his love for you. And, I might add, despite the trauma, you are safe and sound!"

"So what happened to all my praise? I'm the one who gets shoved on a hook, dangled into all sorts of weird situations, and has to get out of it. And you're on his side!"

"Gosh, you're a tricky one. As soon as you can't win, you try to make me feel sorry for you. Pan asked you to trust him. Of your own choice, you did. So stop grumbling. He didn't say it would be easy, did he?"

Grudgingly, I surrendered. "Okay, okay. You're right."

"And one more thing," she declared. "While you persist in being reluctant and negative, you are still part of that storm!"

I spent the remainder of the day reading, although speculating on the night's events occupied much of my time. I acknowledged that the mystical whiteness and blackness of the storm had a counterpart in every human Being. The negativity I had encountered was indeed partly my own, magnified and amplified by that of countless other people. But I had not been engulfed. As a surfer would say, I hadn't wiped out!

Early the following morning, I headed for the river. As I walked beneath the huge outstretched branches of the Morton Bay fig tree, large, crisp, sun-dried leaves crackled beneath my feet and sunlight burst with tiny explosions of heat onto my shoulders. I had hoped to catch a glimpse of a platypus foraging in the river for a late breakfast, but I was out of luck. The surface of the water was dark; the deep, early-morning shade had subtly altered the mood of the river. Scarcely a ripple broke the water's tranquil surface.

I walked out onto the end of my board and dived. The cool water closed over me. I floated very gently and slowly to the surface, my eyes just clearing the water, and noticed a huge bronze dragonfly perched on a spike of sedge grass only inches from my face. I stayed unmoving, captivated by the beauty of this superb, biologically perfect creature.

I chilled quickly in the water, so I climbed from the river to sit on the board in the warm sun. Impossibly, Pan sat next to me. He wore the same faded greens, and was again a normal size. Looking into his eyes, for the first time I felt comfortable without needing him to *make* me feel at ease. And I knew what the difference was!

"I suppose you know all about my little outburst to Treenie?" I asked. "I meant it, every single word! Do you know what really bugged me? You asked me to trust your love for me. That gave me confidence, but then I felt betrayed! Going into that storm was the worst nonphysical experience I have ever had. I felt totally lost."

"I know all that, Michael, and I do love you. I consider you a most courageous person. Once thrown in, you respond magnificently. One thing, however—you do not know what *lost* is."

I ignored the last remark; it did not seem important.

"Tell me, did you listen to my altercation with Treenie?"

"Of course. I hope you heed what she said. I even prompted her with a few suggestions." His mouth curved into a sly smile, tiny shards of light flashing from his eyes.

Despite my indignation, I had to laugh. "You're absolutely impossible."

"Only if you believe in impossibilities, Michael. And luckily, despite all your truculence, you do not!"

"What was the point of throwing me into that storm?"

"Michael! I have told you before, I know you better than

you know yourself. You *know* the purpose. Suppose you tell me!"

I frowned in thought, seeking to sum up the essence of what I had learned. "The strongest impression I have now — having had a chance to simmer down — is that human negativity is a creative force. I had always assumed that anger, bitterness, greed, and our other negative feelings merely dissipated when they left us, somehow dispersed into nothingness. It's a real eye-opener to learn that such energy builds into a destructive force that is eventually expressed in violence."

"What else?"

"Well, it's rather shocking to learn that that negative energy can only be expressed by returning to its point of origin. I had no idea that cause and effect worked within atmospheric levels. Knowing that our mental garbage can accumulate in the atmosphere and then be dumped back on us in the destructive fury of a storm is rather frightening. It's the sow-and-reap effect! Just imagine the effect if we could create that much love and joy!"

"That *is* the human potential. And?"

"By yielding to my own inner negative fears, I conquered them. Without doubt, negativity is born from all our many little fears, and those fears destroy the quality of our lives. Yet I'm not really aware of surrendering. I don't feel I did anything."

"That is the whole essence. You did nothing. If you had tried to surrender, you would have created resistance, for surrender is a 'letting go,' not something you can force. By 'giving in,' you give to your inner self."

We sat in silence. I wanted to digest what he had said, while Pan was happy playing with blue wrens.

I was so lost in thought that Pan's next words caught me by surprise. "You have made many journeys out of your body, but each time it is I who have taken you out."

"Taken! *Blasted* is the operative word," I said laughing. "You rip me out of my physical body."

"Yes, well, I'll teach you a rather unique method. You can exit the body by certain excellent meditation techniques, but I have a method that you may enjoy. Maybe then you will not need my assistance."

"I'm all for that. Your last effort nearly dislocated my neck."

Pan laughed in delight. "Yes, it was a mighty snatch, even if I do say so. Now, to business. You are about to learn the Pan method of leaving your physical body."

He pointed to the base of the old bridge board where it was lodged under a small shelf of rock. "Sit on the board so that your feet are firmly on the ground."

I did so.

"When I say one, you stand up, two, you sit down, three up, four down, and so on. When I reach eleven, your physical body remains seated, but your inner consciousness leaps up . . . and out! Ready?"

"One!"

I stood up.

"Two!"

I sat down.

"Three!"

I stood up.

"No. No. When I say stand, I mean leap up with total

abandon. Up, up, as though reaching for the sky. And sit down with a heavy thud. Right. Try it again."

"One!"

I leaped up energetically.

"Two!"

I collapsed back.

"Three!"

I leaped up enthusiastically.

"Four!"

I thudded back onto the board.

This continued until . . . "Eleven!"

My spiritual self leaps upwards, soaring out of my physical body with ease. I am up and out!

"That was easy enough. You did well. The Pan technique seldom fails, once mastered!"

He is mocking, but it is a thrill to be walking in a body that although appearing normal, is made of light, is weightless. And to be walking along the surface of the river—with Pan—is something else!

Because I am wide awake, I am aware of both physical self and nonphysical self. The former remains calm and relaxed, while the latter moves into a different mode of experience. Both aspects of self are integrated into a single conscious experience.

I am lighter than mist as I move down the river, and my visual impressions come from an all-embracing inner seeing. Moving rainbows of light cling to trees, bushes, and every blade of grass. Everything is transformed by light and color into a subtle vibration. I am aware that this kaleidoscope of color and light somehow lives, is part of Nature, blending and exchanging energies in the endless movement we call life and death. All the living creatures of the riverside are contained in this fluid light, some individually, some as a group.

The water on which my light self hovers no longer clings to the riverbed. No longer is it controlled by physical laws. Instead, it flows in multidimensional layers of visual sound, a stream in which I can faintly perceive other Beings. Some of them see Pan, and when they do their light presence glows brighter, as though influenced by some powerful energy source. Briefly they look at me, and I feel there is a registering of surprise among them. To perceive other Beings that are composed of light and to try to decipher them in human terms is not easy, especially when a feeling of otherness accompanies their obvious intelligence.

How long Pan and I flowed in total harmony with the life of that multidimensional river reality, I have no idea. In human terms, the experience lasted no more than thirty minutes.

Under Pan's direction, we returned to the board on which I sat. I felt my physical body take a long, deep breath as my light, nonphysical body merged with it. I felt dense! After an experience of such lightness, my body felt heavy and cumbersome. I actually felt that I was resuming a nonreal state, that this was not my natural body or my natural state of Beingness.

Pan glanced at me in approval. "Your perception is correct. The total time you spend in a physical body is only a fraction of your experience of Being. You spend far more time outside the human reality as you understand it than in it. Of course, in reality there is only no-time."

I looked into his golden eyes. "Pan, how did I get into the Guidestone in my original experience? My physical body locked, while my nonphysical body was literally drawn out. Were you involved in that?"

"I helped. Let us say that your Greater Self set up the timing and the situation, while I assisted. I switched off one reality, and switched on another. You did the rest. You put your self into the Guidestone, not me."

I could accept that. After all I had since experienced, I was beginning to realize that my human potential was very considerable. But I had another question. "What *is* the Guidestone? It certainly isn't just an average stone."

"No, far from it. The Guidestone is a stone of power. Some are natural in Nature, but some are primed by Beings. The Guidestone was one of the latter."

My mind boggled.

Pan jumped onto the end of the board in one bound. Again, he leaped high into the air, the board whipping him up as though it had flexed under half a ton of weight. As he vanished, his words, in total conflict with all logic and reason, continued to emanate from where he had been sitting.

"You have done well, Michael. Be happy."

122

I swam again, but I no longer felt the magic in the river. Still I stayed, knowing I had to accept physical reality as the major part of my daily life. Whatever my mission was on Earth, it required my physical self. I thought about Pan's last words: be happy. Yes, I felt happy. Despite a bumpy journey, I had experienced the inner realms of plant, mineral, and animal consciousness. I had been within the essence of water and had entered a storm. And I had emerged from all of it unscathed, even if badly shaken. Each mystical experience connected with the previous one, rather like the beads on a necklace. By commencing with water, I had gained an overall impression of the whole, for water is in all life forms, even rock! The plant kingdom had revealed that a physical act, such as the spraying of toxins, in one small place has an effect on the whole. The mineral kingdom revealed both how we have each become concretized in our separation from one another and the potential of the whole. The animal kingdom revealed my inability to love myself and how I judged myself. It also showed that none of the animals involved judged me. Nature does not judge.

I stared up river, wondering what awaited me. Each experience revealed to me a greater view of myself and the way I and every other human fitted into the overall pattern of life. Pan was showing me that the nonphysical aspect of Nature and humanity had many hidden ramifications. I was learning that to find out "who I am" required that I embrace not only the me I *think* I know, but also my mystical self. The unknown outweighed the known, but paradoxically I could not make the unknown known. I could only experience, learn, and accept. This was the path into the Beyond, and I knew now that the membrane at the Door to Beyond would never yield until I knew who I was.

Pan had often told me that he knew me better than I knew myself. I believed him now. Even though I had chosen the mystic path of Nature, Pan was designing this journey. I realized, with some irony, that I now trusted him implicitly.

When a yellow and gold butterfly settled on my towel only seconds before I reached for it, its wings opening and closing in flashing golden winks, I knew that Pan was still nearby.

7
Becoming Dolphin

"You will have to leave all this."

I stared upriver, my eyes moist. That I was attached to the river was acutely obvious. A week had passed since Pan had taught me how to leap out of my physical body, and each day I had spent hours on my old bridge board. Evening shadows were stretching dark, elongated fingers across the water when Pan made his appearance. We chatted for a while before Pan dropped his bombshell.

"Why? Why do I have to move from here?"

"Having acknowledged your fixation, the reason should be obvious. You must withdraw your roots from dear old Mother Earth. You must become a free spirit on this planet, not attached to it. You cannot remain fixed and go Beyond."

"So where do Treenie and I go from here?"

"Life will present your next home at the perfect time. All you need for assisting the process is trust."

"Will you be able to find me if we move from here?" I asked rather anxiously.

Pan tilted his head back, laughing uproariously. When he turned those golden eyes on me and blinked, I noticed that the light in them illuminated his eyelids. The evening dusk made the effect quite startling, rather Halloweenish.

"Michael, I could find you anywhere."

"That's comforting to know."

He only smiled, while my fascination with his illumined eyes took my thoughts elsewhere.

"It may surprise you to learn that your next connection is with an intelligent species."

"But humans are the only intelligent species on Earth," I began, and then I realized my error. "You mean the dolphins, don't you?"

"That is exactly who I mean."

"But I have tried to connect with dolphins dozens of times. Treenie and I sometimes see them on our beach walks, and, no matter how hard I try to communicate, nothing happens!"

Pan dismissed my comments with an elegant wave of his hand. "As always, it's simply a matter of timing!"

Only a few days later, Lance Rose, our landlord, told Treenie and me that he had been offered a good price for the riverside property we'd been living on. He had not even considered selling, so the offer came as a surprise. Because of a prior agreement, he offered the property to us first. He was keen for us to buy it, for we had become good friends and he enjoyed paying visits to the place where he and his wife, Enid, had spent much of their lives.

"You go ahead and sell," I said with some reluctance. "Treenie and I feel it's time we moved out of the valley. Given the choice, we would like a place with some elevation."

Treenie and I realized that life was indeed saying "move on," so a few weeks later we set out on a journey into southern Queensland. At this stage, we decided to look not for a home but simply for an area where the vibrations were right for us. Staying with friends on each leg of the journey, we moved from one place to another, finally deciding on a particularly exotic and pleasing location. Feeling happy with the results of our search, we drove homewards, calling on our good friends Mike and Rosemary Nicholas in Brisbane to stay the night and share our news.

"Did you go and have a look on Kiel Mountain?" asked Mike. "It's very close to the place you like and really beautiful. You'd love it."

I looked at Treenie uncertainly. "The name's familiar. Have we ever been there?"

"We were there about six years ago, very briefly."

I have a bad memory for places, and couldn't remember the place at all. Also, I had no intention of going back to look at any mountain. We were very satisfied with the area we had chosen.

Next day we drove home.

During our trip away, the expected sale had fallen flat. Nevertheless, we felt that life was prompting us to make the move. Still, with the pressure off, we decided to take our time. A few days later, a man I was talking with casually of our trip said, "Ah! I know that area very well. Did you go and have a look at Kiel Mountain while you were there? It's a really beautiful place to live."

I looked at him in surprise. "Funny you should say that. Someone else also suggested we should have looked up there."

Three weeks later, Russell, our youngest son phoned to

say he'd met the daughter of a friend of ours. The girl asked about us, and in the course of the conversation she mentioned a house for sale—a house on top of Kiel Mountain!

"I think you'd better give me that phone number, Russ. And thanks," I said.

I told Treenie about the conversation. "Life is saying Kiel Mountain loud and clear. Three times should be enough for anybody!" I was enthusiastic.

"I think you'd better phone and get some details," she suggested.

I did. I was told that Kiel Mountain was reputed to be a power point on a ley line. Ley lines are to the planet what meridian lines are to our bodies. Many old European churches, cathedrals, and monasteries were built on ley lines, and it is said that power accumulates at certain points. I was also told that the small mountain was only a few minutes' drive from the sea and that the climate was mild, without extremes in heat or humidity. The unnamed property was two acres of open forest right on top of the mountain. All in all, the place sounded like paradise, and the photographs that arrived by post a few days later appeared to confirm it.

When we visited the property, we found it to be simply perfect. From the moment Treenie and I first set foot on the drive leading down to the house tucked in among the gum trees—by mutual consent—it was ours.

The transaction went without a hitch. We were due to take possession in one month.

Packing made the month pass quickly. On the last day, I could not leave without saying farewell to my beloved river. I had a heavy heart as I went slowly and carefully down the steep steps. They were wet and slippery from recent heavy rains.

I was in for a shock! My bridge board was gone! A week of heavy rain had produced a flood; at its peak, flowing fast and very powerfully, the river had taken my old bridge board . . . my old and faithful friend. How strange life is. Shortly after we had moved to this place six years earlier, a flood had deposited the old, washed-out bridge board onto the rocks where I now sat. Now, in the manner it had brought the huge, heavy board to me, the river had as easily removed it. What uncanny timing! I felt, then, that the river had welcomed me with the board and now it was saying farewell.

As I watched, gently undulating shoals of tiny brown fish clustered near the rocks where I sat. A fantail flew from a twig above my head, swooping to the water's surface to catch an insect before flying onto a drooping frond of wild palm grass. The vivid splash of black and white bird on dark green foliage was the perfect art of Nature. Despite the bird's tiny weight, the slender stem dipped alarmingly toward the river, down and down in response to its diminutive burden. I watched the fantail's antics with a feeling akin to envy. The bird was so free, so sure of each movement, so totally in the moment. The fantail's only concern was food—and in that it was certainly not alone! Beneath the bird, a small rock dragon scampered over the drying remains of flood debris, its jaws snapping as it pounced on first one March fly, then another. Smaller and skinnier than its water dragon cousin, its head twisted as though on an endless swivel, the rock dragon kept watch on me while pursuing its prey.

Another fantail flew in on a nervous blur of wings, and for a few breathless seconds the pair of birds sat close to each other, beaks almost touching in a moment's intimacy, before their fluttering, uncontainable energy took them deeper into the wild palm grass.

I dived, frolicked, and swam, coming to terms with my leave-taking. When I emerged from the cold water, a twig fell from the treetops and splashed into the water before me. I looked up to see a pair of pale gray herons on long, stilt legs perched on a high branch of a river oak.

This was one of those moments of natural elegance when everything comes together with serendipitous grace. The great bronze dragonfly, by no means a common visitor, zoomed past with an aura of majesty, while the river formed small, gasping whirlpools as it flowed powerfully over the submerged rocks.

A lonely gray feather riding high on the water had completed several ineffectual circuits from the rippled edge of the open flow back into an inlet when a slight gust of breeze took it skimming across the surface onto the current of the main stream. I watched as it began its journey downriver, a single gray feather facing the unknown, no longer part of a heron's plumage. The message was clear. Time to go!

Our first week on Kiel Mountain was all frenzied activity. Treenie, who had shed her tears as we departed our home by the river, was a bundle of organized energy. I had departed in high spirits but was feeling totally misplaced. I had looked forward to living in the house but now found it impersonal, like a motel. And the mountain was achingly devoid of a river—my river!

It was not until I realized I was looking for the river each day that I finally came to terms with our parting. Deliberately, I turned my attention to accepting and appreciating the particular beauty of our new home. And there was beauty in abundance. Gray gums, which shed their bark each year, astounded us with the deep ochre-orange coloring of their new trunks when wet. Also, there was a great peace on the mountain, perfect for a writer, and if Nature was less flamboyant than by the river, it was no less active. While we now had no platypus to grace a river, we had the echidna, a marsupial spiny anteater, to wander our garden of trees. Still, it wasn't until a yellow and gold butterfly slowly winked its delicate wings from the edge of our swimming pool one sunny morning that I knew I had made the adjustment!

One day our mail produced a letter from the west coast of Australia. Christine Olsen and Keith Nightingale had purchased and read *Talking With Nature* and, having felt a great affinity with it, invited Treenie and me to do a series of workshops in their area. With uncanny foresight, they offered me the perfect bait—if we wished, they would take us to Monkey Mia for a few days!

I did not know Christine or Keith, but I did know of Monkey Mia! I had been wanting to go there for years and had been waiting for the right opportunity. This was surely it! We accepted the invitation, and at the appointed time flew to Perth.

A sign on a bag carrier read, "Welcome Michael and Treenie," and in no time we were firm friends with Jack and Barbara Bailey, our hosts in Perth. Workshops and talks came and went, and the time to visit Monkey Mia arrived. Monkey Mia is no more than an isolated caravan park in Shark Bay. Situated hundreds of miles from anywhere in a bleak, inhospitable landscape that could easily belong to another planet, its one redeeming factor is the group of wild dolphins that voluntarily meets there with hundreds of people every day.

Our group consisted of Christine, Keith, and their delightful eighteen-month-old baby, Amy, a couple of their friends, Marie and Sonia, and Treenie and me. We took a car, plus their Landrover and caravan. The two-day drive north of Perth is an unrelieved, straight coast road that seems endless, but thoughts of the dolphins interspersed with flashes of color from Western Australia's incredible and strange native wildflowers made the trip pass very quickly. Unfortunately, we were too early for the full wildflower display, and only caught mere hints of the glory to unfold in another couple of months.

At the appropriate junction, we left the main coast road to drive another hundred miles or so along the peninsula on which Monkey Mia is located. Finally, in a cloud of red dust, we pulled into the overcrowded caravan park to find our prebooked site.

There are only two reasons for visiting Monkey Mia: to fish and to see the dolphins! Of course, without fish there would be no dolphins, and the fishing is famed for its excellence. Because of its sheltered position, the bay is predominantly calm, the water seldom disturbed by large waves. Golden sand, unlike the usual white sand of our shoreline, stretches endlessly along the lonely beaches. Seen from one of the nearby low hillocks, the caravan park is an ugly sprawl of caravans intruding into the natural sweep of beauty. Stark, dry, and desertlike, the vista of Shark Bay is outstanding. But the visitors are required to accept this area on its own terms, not imposing their own. When they do, the beauty shines through, overwhelming the initial impression that this is a barren land. It is indeed a place of contrasts, harsh and hot, of prickles, burrs, and thorns, yet the flowers that grace these well-defended plants are soft, delicate, and unique.

A flotilla of small fishing boats bobs gently on the undulating sea, while pelicans fly among them in a stately grace. Along the shoreline there are people, old and young, wealthy and poor, fat and thin—people who appear to have nothing in common. There are probably as many visitors from overseas as from our own fair land, yet despite the obvious diversity one common factor unifies them all: they are here for the dolphins.

After setting up our tent and caravan, we had our meal and retired for the night. It was midwinter, so it was cold despite the midday warmth. Next morning I arrived on the

134

beach just before 7 A.M., eager for my first physical contact with the dolphins. I was alone; the beach and sea were cold and deserted. Minutes later the sun appeared, rising blood red over a low bank of clouds. A snort among the fishing boats announced the arrival of the dolphins. I waded in, calling softly. Five dolphins came cruising up from the greenish depths to the knee-deep shallows. The leading female offered me a small wisp of sea grass. As I took the gift from her, she rolled slightly to one side, making deliberate visual contact with me with a pinkish-red eye. I was instantly aware that this was an intelligent species, and Pan's words came flooding back: "Your next connection is with an intelligent species." I stared at her, awed by the obvious intelligence of her appraisal. She showed none of the normal discomfort an animal exhibits when held by a prolonged stare, only a keen curiosity and hints of deep awareness. By placing the wisp of sea grass in my hand, she had thrilled me beyond measure. I felt the keen pleasure of a child handed an unexpected gift.

Having learned from our eye contact all she needed to know, the dolphin rolled onto her side, presenting herself in a mute invitation I could not ignore. Wonder coursed through me as I stroked her warm, wet-rubber skin. What a privilege. The connection was a thrill far beyond anything I had anticipated. I would have walked all those miles from Perth for a moment such as this!

Within minutes, other early dolphin lovers had spotted our little group, children and adults jostling for attention. Every day people come in their hundreds, some for a few hours, others for days, weeks, and even months. From daybreak to dusk, from fifty to several hundred people throng the beach and shallows, hands reaching out to the dolphins, eager to connect with these amicable and patient creatures from the sea. And every person who approaches the dolphins is given careful scrutiny, as though the dolphins can see into each individual's inner being. Even where a hundred people compete for the attention of half a dozen dolphins, when a stranger walks down to the edge of the sea, a dolphin will look over the newcomer.

Later in the morning, I carried a folding chair onto the small jetty close by the stretch of dolphin beach. I was ready now for a deeper connection—if it happened!—a linking of consciousness on the level of Spirit.

For a while I watched the scene before me: people reaching and stroking, and squealing with excitement, their faces smiling, cameras clicking, a ranger patroling the water to ensure the dolphins' safety. On the dolphins' side were the permanent smiles, gray hides, and flashing tails. The creatures cruised up and down along a hundred-yard stretch of beach in water no more than knee-deep to a human; it was a startling demonstration of trust.

The jetty was thronged with people, so I decided against Pan's method of exiting the body! Instead, I allowed my awareness of self to expand slowly past my physical senses. Even as the process unfolded, I was, surprisingly, aware of a definite surge of assistance from Pan, causing a spiritual reality to emerge as my physical reality receded.

I become aware of being engulfed by ocean. Somewhere, a lone dolphin, an elderly female, is dying. I know this clearly for I can feel her—I *am* her, though only partly. I know she is aware of me, and even in her final moments she willingly shares her reality with me. It is almost as though she has expected me! I feel her lungs expand one last time as she takes a final deep breath of air, and I see through her eyes as she takes a last look at the blue, cloud-scudded sky, curiously close and solid, before her body slides smooth and slick beneath the waves as she dives her last dive. No cold forbidding ocean this, but a warm embrace of comfort and great familiarity.

My self is locked with the dolphin as she slides with abandon and grace into the beckoning depths. She is calm and totally purposeful. There is no pain, nothing obviously wrong. Shocked, I feel seawater flood her lungs after she violently expels her last breath, a rush of huge bubbles hastening to the surface far above. Her calmness controls my panic as her physical body, now vacated, slides gently toward the ocean floor.

Confusion overwhelms me. At the precise moment when her consciousness leaves the dolphin body, somewhere else in the vast ocean a powerful ejaculation forces a baby dolphin from its mother's womb into the waiting waters. Immediately, a nurse dolphin ushers it to the surface, where its first breath gushes into its blowhole.

As the death and birth coincide, I feel some essence of the exiting dolphin mix and merge with the newly born one. I feel other dolphin identities in the new dolphin, yet somehow they instantly integrate into a single sense of One. I am bewildered.

Now, consciously linked with the dolphin that has departed its body, I seem to expand swiftly into a faintly golden light, swimming with a freedom and grace akin to flight. The sensation of free flight deepens. I have a feeling of falling but no fear, and we burst through something into an ocean of richly golden, liquid light. On the jetty, I am flooded with joy. Tears fall from my physical eyes and love washes over and through me in wave after exquisite wave. It is an exultation. With a dolphin, I dive in a body of light into a liquid of no more substance than an early morning vapor.

"Where am I?" The words, though silent, are spoken in my mind.

"No place. No place in human terms, but a place of substance. Call it a different layer of reality than the one you've been used to."

I feel shock as I recognize the silent voice. "Pan?" I ask in astonishment.

Only the laughter of wind chimes answers me, a sound strangely at home in this place of wonder.

"That was Pan, yes, but I am not it." There is reverence contained in the dolphin's words.

"Do you know Pan?"

"Why not? We know the Being, but not by that name. The name is an identity tag, meaningless—except for the meaning you humans give it, and that is generally false."

"But how can you know him?"

"Why not?" the dolphin counters. "A Being that moves through realities with total ease is not exclusive to the

138

human experience. We know this Being, but we give it a different name."

"What is that?"

I sense a soft, curious whistle, which rises slightly to curl, hesitate, and end with a sigh. The very sound produces joy. For all its beauty and simplicity, I know the word *Pan* will never again be totally adequate.

For a while there is silence as we absorb the movement of the golden liquid light in which we bathe. Curiously, we are not moving through it; rather, it seems to flow through and around us. I feel that this life, so different from my usual one, is living me, that I am being experienced just as I am experiencing!

I remember the simultaneous death and birth I had witnessed. "How did that happen?" I ask.

Only as the dolphin begins to answer do I realize that I have not defined my question. But the dolphin and I, although separate, are One! Thought is not private.

"A dolphin is different from a human in a way you might find incomprehensible. Humans experience only a single self in each lifetime, while we experience a number of identities in each life."

"I don't understand."

The dolphin continued. "Humans experience life through intellectual processes. Your sense perceptions are relatively undeveloped. But we experience life through heightened, multiple-sense perception, and our intellectual capacity is far less developed."

A light dawned. "So our environment has basically determined the way we have developed?"

"True, except that we *choose* the environment we live in so we can develop what we consider important. The choice is not random."

"Are you suggesting that my presence here now might mean that I was a dolphin once?"

I am saying you have a spiritual connection, as do all humans. We are not separate in consciousness."

There is a long, slow, no-time pause while I digest the implications of what I have learned. I have a feeling that the dolphin's reference to the experiencing of several identities is important, but the *why* of it eludes me. I feel I have something very important to learn here, but I cannot quite grasp it. It has to do with identity, possibly my own identity, of knowing "who I am."

The dolphin's next words could be my own thoughts. "There is a truth here that you must find. Consider your method of searching. Humans must reason to know, but we know simply by perceiving. Perception reveals no error even if it reveals only a fraction of truth, but reason can be in error, can misinterpret its fractional glimpse."

Another long, no-time pause! Without help, without words, I know that this dolphin and human experience combines to be something far greater than each alone. I know that I am here to learn more about myself, for each step along my path to self-realization seems to involve a higher order in Nature's expressions of conscious form. I have been water, mineral, plant, and animal; now, briefly, I am dolphin, an animal with an unmeasured intelligence. Each experience until now felt familiar, but this dolphin shares knowledge with me of which I have no concept.

I have the feeling that *identity* is the big lesson here, plus the ability to learn by perception rather than by reason alone.

"Humans are an immortal expression of Divine Love; identities are a brief expression of human individuality. Perceive the truth in this and you will realize the truth of Self for which you search." The dolphin's words are within me. We are dual, combined, yet very individual. I am neither overwhelmed nor overpowered, and I can leave any time I choose. However, although I share her words, sadly, much of their meaning I hold as knowledge that I cannot interpret. It is beyond me. A scale of Beingness is involved that I cannot fathom. I am acutely aware that my intuitive perception is slight compared with the dolphin's— yet I feel we are equal.

Without any awareness of change, my self has separated from the dolphin's. I see her light body shimmering like silver as she swims in the golden liquid light. Her eyes are on mine and in them I see a clear promise.

Suddenly, I was gazing out of physical eyes at a sleek dolphin swimming among the jostling people. Oddly, the dolphin turned away from all the outstretched hands, and with an incredible burst of speed approached the jetty. For a long moment, our eyes met; then, with surging strength, the dolphin headed out toward the open sea. I wondered if she, or any of the other nearby dolphins, had any knowledge of what had just taken place.

Later that day, I went for a long walk along the curving

bay. Shell rock lay in large slabs on the glistening sand, and the fossilized shells stuck out in a profusion of varieties. As the tide receded, huge stretches of sand were revealed. Oyster catchers sporting black and white plumage and glossy orange beaks pecked them over. A few dozen large pelicans eyed me suspiciously as I strolled past, but I was not enough of a threat to prevent their frenzied preening and cleaning of their flight and chest feathers. Like leaves blowing before a mischievous breeze, sandpipers scuttled over the beach, moving in a thin, ragged wave before me.

I watched Nature as she unveiled her west coast beauty, but my thoughts were elsewhere. I was remembering the ease with which the dolphin had let go of her body at the moment of death. This ease attested to a greater-than-human knowing. There was no choking on that great lungful of water, just a smooth exit. She had surrendered her body with the same ease with which I would emerge from the driving seat of a car—and with no more attachment! It was apparent that death was no mystery to a dolphin.

I marveled then at the simultaneous birth and death. How extraordinary! That any life form could experience more than a single identity at once had never even occurred to me. This was not a group soul; it was an individuality that encompassed more than one. What a contradiction! The dying dolphin had retained its particular identity, while at the same time projecting some part of its consciousness into the baby. I had felt other dolphin identities—as many as six—enter and merge. Were they dying?

"Embrace the reality without too much analysis."

"Pan!" I was so pleased to see him at my side, I turned

to embrace him, but—how strange! He was at my side, but then again he was not! I could see him, but he had no physical substance. Even before I reached out to hold him physically, I knew his solidity was an illusion. "Pan?"

He chuckled, a human sound mingled with distant wind chimes. "This will suffice. I am with you. Disengage your reasoning and allow the essence of your experience to filter across your senses. Allow what is to simply *be*. Not knowing allows access to *knowing*. Reason that!" Wind chimes and laughter drifted from silence into reality.

He continued to walk—or drift—at my side, and it was clear he expected me to stop thinking and . . . to feel? Clarity emerged. Without knowing how I knew, I came to understand how a number of dolphins could share a reality within one physical body. They share a perception of life, experiencing without conclusions. Conclusions do not exist for them. Humans, though, *reason* with life, drawing conclusions. If a number of human psyches were to inhabit a body and reason with life, the result would be chaos, madness. For the dolphins, a shared perception increases the experience and somehow magnifies it. There is no conflict, no confusion.

"You see, all things are possible when you allow the possibility of impossibilities!" Again the laughter, not mocking, but so filled with joy and love that tears filled my eyes.

"But, Pan, what about those things the dolphin told me?"

"What do you . . . feel?"

"I don't know. I really don't. The meaning is so far beyond my experience. I just don't know."

"Wonderful. Another opportunity for knowing through not knowing."

I sighed, releasing the problem. It would just have to wait for some other . . . and again came clarity!

The death and exit had been smooth and familiar, the dolphin totally at ease, in control. She "knew" what to expect. The golden sea of light had been as much—or more—home than the physical ocean that housed her physical body. Generally, we humans do not know what to expect of death, and the death experience therefore varies according to our spiritual development. By sharing perception through an individual, the dolphins shared a spiritual evolvement. As *one* knew, they *all* knew.

The ocean of golden mist existed on another level of reality. It seemed to be a place of deliberate synthesis, where the merging of two streams of consciousness created a greater wholeness in each individual stream than the single experience did, or could.

The number of individual dolphins and humans involved was comparatively small, but it felt deliberate. I was aware that it was not an experience exclusive to me, for in the ocean of light I could feel other participants. In terms of Wholeness, the experience of the few became the experience of the All, even if not every individual was conscious of it. Consciousness is One. As humans, our individuality separates us from each other. Dolphins experience the individual on a shared basis: thus, individuality is synthesized into a holistic experience. Oneness!

The differences between dolphins and humans loomed large to me . . . and then receded. We were as different as earth and water, and yet as close as brothers and sisters.

Later that evening, I shared my experience with the others in our group. They accepted it easily. Still, I felt the need for confirmation. My experience was so outrageous alongside the little dolphin literature I had read, I was very hesitant to share it any further.

Early on our fifth morning at Monkey Mia, Treenie and I went for a walk along the beach. We talked of our time with the dolphins. After about three-quarters of an hour, Treenie turned back, but I continued to walk. As I strolled on, I tried to communicate my need for confirmation to the dolphins, but I heard and felt nothing. Some two and a half hours later, I arrived back at the caravan park to be met on the beach by an excited Treenie.

"What do you think?" she called out as I approached. "A mother dolphin came in about an hour ago with a new baby." She paused, her eyes sparkling. "The rangers estimate that it is five days old."

"Oh," I said blankly. "That's nice."

"Don't you see?" exploded Treenie. "You had the experience of the dolphin's death and birth five days ago. This confirms it for you. If the mother dolphin had come in tomorrow, it would have been too late."

Treenie beamed at me while it all slowly registered.

"Wake up. We leave first thing tomorrow. The dolphin has met your need," she said patiently.

While Treenie went to make me some coffee, I walked over to the crowds, excitedly pointing at the new baby. I stared in wonder as mother and baby swam among the people in total trust. The baby was maybe four feet long, a perfect replica of its mother. As they cruised close, I reached out, stroking the baby as it briefly detached itself from its mother's side. Instantly, I knew that this was the baby whose birth I had experienced. In that moment, I felt the familiar presence of a female dolphin swimming with a body of light in a golden ocean of mist—and swimming in the baby body in a physical ocean by the mother's side.

"It gives us joy to meet your need of confirmation. We acknowledge that it was neither doubt nor lack of acceptance that created your need, but a sincere desire to represent us in a truthful manner." Fleetingly swift, the words flowed through my mind, highlighted by the presence of the dolphin of light. Then the words faded into the "oooh's" and "aaah's" of human admiration as the little dolphin bobbed in the sea beside its mother's sleek body. And within a few minutes, the two had gone, heading out to join the large school of dolphins playing offshore.

I sighed with pleasure. When Treenie and I had come to Monkey Mia, I had had no expectations of any exceptional happenings. I had come content to see and stroke wild dolphins; anything else was a bonus. The last thing I had expected was Pan—and that the dolphins knew him seemed extraordinary. As always, my experience had been another step along my path, but the reality of self-realization and stepping through the membrane into Beyond still seemed remote. I had learned from the animal consciousness to cease judging myself, and I had experienced the dogs' unconditional love for me, but, alas, perfect self-acceptance defeated me. Knowing about the need for unconditional love was important, but to actualize this knowledge

146

was vital to my progress. Now I had learned that individuality in a dolphin can include a number of separate identities. Wow! I was aware of being locked into my present identity, but how could I possibly break free? This identity *is* me, but it's only my personal self. I wanted the Greater Self. Is that some other me? The dolphin had given me a clue where it—I?—was, but I was helpless to pursue it. I sighed, perplexed. All I could do was allow Pan to teach me in his mystical way. I had once said he was my guru; well, I would trust him. That, at least, I had learned!

8
Entering Another Realm

"Am I ready to enter the Guidestone again and walk through the Door?"

Pan shook his head absently, his eyes cast up into the branches high above.

"But why? I've experienced all the realms of Nature you said I needed to explore. I've learned many lessons, so what's stopping me?"

He pointed up into the branches of the tree against which I was leaning. "That is so beautiful," he murmured. Curious, I stared up into the tree, following the line of each branch and limb and looking in vain for the creature that was evoking his admiration and attention. Systematically, my eyes searched the tree, but I could find nothing. Defeated, I asked, "What is?"

He turned toward me, his golden dome of a head seeming to reflect the rising golden sun. "Look at the leaves outlined against the sky. Watch the play of their movement. They live."

I gazed up into the tree again. Ah, yes! He was right. Now I could see and appreciate the movement of beautifully sculptured gray-green leaves set against the clear blue sky. Maybe it was a breeze in the upper branches, but each leaf was moving as though separately animated, engaging in active conversation with its neighbor.

"*That's* why."

"Uh! Why what?"

"Why you are not yet ready."

"What! Just because I didn't notice the leaves in the way you did?"

"No. Because you are so preoccupied with form you do not perceive the formless. The leaves you so glibly dismiss as waving in the breeze are, in fact, animated by other forces that you should have remembered."

I frowned in perplexity.

"Relive. Remember."

Starting with the dolphin encounter, I fumblingly worked my way back through the range of extraordinary experiences that Pan had opened for me. When I eventually recalled the blackberry experience, reliving the relationship between blackberry and tiny Beings, I understood the connection. "So what happens now?"

"You have connected with another form of intelligent physical life. Now you must renew and expand your connections with metaphysical intelligence on this planet."

"Gee! Is there no end to this?"

"That is for you to decide."

"I didn't mean it."

Pan chuckled mischievously. "Are you ready?"

In my haste, words tumbled out. "Hang-on-a-minute-before-you-do-one-of-your-snatches. Let me jump out." I was breathless.

His smile was a delight. "I planned to."

Vigorously, I jumped up and sat down heavily a few times. Then suddenly I was up and out.

Rather to my astonishment, I am balancing on the slender twigs of a fallen branch. Whereas they would normally be crushed flat by my weight, I am easily supported a couple of feet above the ground. I am aware of light around my body, which is glowing from some inner source. It occurs to me that I am that light.

When I step off the twigs, my weightlessness opens up a whole new experience. I lift up my arms and float gently upward, hovering as I hold my arms out at shoulder level. Timelessness is obvious; I can feel it. No aging mars this wondrous realm. There's no hurry to do, no hurry to finish, just a timeless sense of Being.

I look at the tree through eyes that are undoubtedly my own but that must normally be closed. Imagine my dilemma. I am trying to describe something that is metaphysical with words that have been created for a physical reality. The tree on which I feast my eyes is both physical and more than physical. To say it is beautiful is trite. It is something beyond our classification of beauty; it is *alive* in a way far beyond our understanding of that word. Take the fallen branch on which I am standing as an example. By normal definitions, it is dead, a lifeless branch, yet I now see it as seething with energy. Although it is no longer animated by the life sap of the tree, it is nevertheless vibrant with a life not dependent on the growing tree. Despite a process of decay, the "dead" wood is a force field within itself, host to an incredible array of tiny, almost transparent Beings.

And the tree from which it fell! In normal terms, the tree is just another gum tree, without any particular beauty of shape or foliage. But in this realm it is breathtaking. It is a living rainbow moving as a column from the Earth, flowing into the shape of the physical tree. The rainbow of energy is enclosed in a sheath of vibrant, white, motionless motion.

"Nice, huh?"

"Nice! *Nice* doesn't get close." I turn expectantly toward Pan, but he is not with me. Instead, I am gazing upon an elf, a classic elf of the type I read of as a child, except for one thing: it is easily three feet tall!

"No good looking for Pan. I am your guide in this realm."

"Oh, er . . . thank you."

"You are not frightened, are you?"

"No. I don't think I am. Just a bit disconcerted."

"Oh. Why?"

"Several reasons. For one thing, I didn't know elves could be so tall. Also, while Pan is nothing like I ever imagined, you're a classic fairy tale elf. That's odd, to put it mildly. Even your clothes are classic elf costume." I have to smile. "You're a nonsurprising surprise!"

The elf laughs, a sound startlingly reminiscent of wind chimes, and I feel suspicious. "You're not Pan having me on, are you?"

More laughter, echoed by a myriad of tiny Beings smaller than damsel flies. They fly around my head, diving into my aura of light with obvious enjoyment. I have the impression that they are swimming in my Being in much the same way that I swam in the river.

"Really! I am not Pan. He is an entity unto himself."

Bemused, I gaze again at the elf. My impression is of neither male nor female. The elf is of both sexes while being neither! It is wearing a small green skull cap set on fine yellow curls. A dark green, skin-tight tunic encloses it from neck to wrists and ankles. On its tiny, slender feet are pointed brown boots. The face now regarding me with amused tolerance is beautiful—the features are delicate yet stamped with strength. The nose is tiny, exquisitely molded above small, clearly defined lips. Blue eyes of great intensity meet my own, and I feel connected to this Being in a way I do not understand. The most ridiculous question surfaces in my mind. How did it get those clothes on? No zips, no buttons! The elf and the clothes are not separate. Odd.

My thoughts must be as transparent as ever!

"I do not put these clothes on, I draw them to me. I can draw any form to me I wish . . . within certain limits. I do not put clothes on; they just *are*. I drew this form from you, from your impression of elves."

Aha! That explains a lot. "So you can be something else if you wish?"

Instantly, the elf disappears, but in a blink a faun about the same height and build is standing in its place. This is another delightful Being. Its head combines that of a child and a kid; it is blended in an utterly natural way. I can see why children are called kids, so completely natural is this faun. Again, it is a classic. The body is that of a boy; the legs and feet are a kid's.

"Do you like me?"

"I think you are wonderful. I *love* you." I am surprised, but it is the simple truth.

The faun vanishes, to be replaced by the elf. "Which do you prefer?"

"Do you mean I have a choice?"

"If you need to choose."

"I don't. Any form you want to take suits me. Even though you change form, your energy remains the same. I'm not sure how I do it, but I recognize the essential you."

In a blink, the elf vanishes once more, to be replaced by a twinkling light about the size of a ping-pong ball. "Are you comfortable with me now?" The words come in the same manner of inner hearing, and I can feel the Beingness of the light.

"Yes, absolutely. But do you have a name?"

"Not in humanese. You give me one."

"How about Ping?"

"I like it. Any more questions?"

"No."

"Then you are ready."

"Ready for the Door?" I ask excitedly.

"Oh, good heavens, no. Ready for our realm, is what I mean."

"But aren't I in your realm?"

A thin chuckle comes from Ping. "To coin a phrase from your own mind, you ain't seen nothing yet!"

"Oh! So where do we go from here?"

Ping is flying around me, a flashing circle of twinkling light. "We are only on the periphery of my realm, sort of half in yours and half in mine. Follow me and do as I tell you."

I notice a huge orb of pale silver light not far away. How it got there or where it came from I do not know. It looks rather as though the moon has fallen to Earth, and though it is opaque, it is verging on transparent. Ping is already flying toward it and, after only a moment's hesitation, I follow. I am half floating, half flying. I realize that when Pan took me onto the river he must have helped me move around without my knowing it. I feel a bit wobbly as I follow Ping, but my control rapidly improves.

As I pass through the silver orb, I feel a brief chill penetrate my Beingness; then it is gone. What I see, feel, am, is sheer wonder. Although it is still daylight, the light is silver, rather than sunlight. Soft, subtle shades of glowing light cast shadows unlike normal shadows. The shadows here are somehow transparent and wraithlike, highlighting rather than subduing whatever they fall upon. The light is fascinating—it comes from within rather than without, and is clearly an energy. I am aware that normal Earth light is energy, but this is different—you can *feel* this light. My whole body is tingling with light. Light is my substance, my food, my drink, even my breath.

I am not breathing; there is no need. This light is everything I need, everything I am. I can feel this light as my Beingness and, even more wonderfully, I can feel my Beingness in the light. Where this light shines and illuminates this ethereal realm, I am.

I am Ping, an experience of Being that is extraordinarily different from humanness, yet it contains the same notes of a cosmic song. Our inner melody is One, but the singer and the song are very different.

Before me is a small, radiant-green hill. I could say illu-mined-green or living-green and each term would be ac-curate. Beyond the hill, everything is shrouded in silver light; there is no distant vision. All is here and now. What I see is what I am involved in; there is nothing else. Small trees, amazing trees, are growing on the hill. The phys-ical tree is clearly apparent, yet within and without are other dimensions of tree. Within is a similar flowing, spread-ing stretch of rainbow light permeated by countless num-bers of bee-sized Beings of intense light. I cannot see any form to them, just light . . . and energy. But, oh, what energy! Simply standing near these myriad Beings is rather like taking a blast of heatless energy, as in the chamber in the Guidestone.

"Without their assistance, there could be no trees." Ping's voice is with me, his own light body close by. Of course, what I am seeing is not really seen! It is a totality of spiritual absorption. In some inexplicable manner, I am all that is happening in this realm. I do not see it—I *am* it. Beyond that, I cannot explain.

The tiny specks of energy, Nature Spirits, are zipping in and out of the tree. Obviously, to them the physical tree is of a substance no denser than the rainbow light. But there is more to this. I see another Being that both con-tains and is contained in the tree. I am aware that to separate them is to cause the tree's death, yet the Spirit of the tree is eternal, immortal. And so also is the tree. Whether the tree is physically cut down or dies of old age, the physical tree and the Spirit of tree are one and the same. Death is the great illusion of physical reality. This

Being, often called a Deva, has an influence stretching beyond the physical reach of the tree. I can feel it. All trees of a species are contained within the ethereal body of a Deva spirit, no matter how physically separated they may be.

I feel approval from Ping as I and the Deva merge in consciousness. In this realm, there is only here and now; all else is shrouded in a silver nothingness. The same is true of the reality of Deva Spirit. With respect to the Spirit, distance and time do not exist. The Earth is no more than the palm of my hand, the beginning and end no more or less than Now. This is the Deva's reality. Even the hill contains and is contained by a Spirit Being, one that differs from that of the tree inasmuch as Deva connects tree with air while the Rock Spirit connects tree with Earth. And the trees? They are a pipeline of Energy connecting the stars with Earth, essential to our well-being, our balance, and universal vision.

Ping moves to the hill, pausing at its summit. As I follow, a whole new scenario opens before me. Different types of Nature Spirits are massed upon the hilltop. There are many hundreds of elves all moving around with a purpose and order that is somehow both poetic and confusing. All have an overriding quality of gentleness and fairness. Hovering above the elves are tiny patterns of light weaving in and out of a self-contained spiral. As I watch, I see they are minute, transparent forms as elegant as . . . fairies! Enthralled, I watch them winking—they are tiny transparent fairies. Then they are intense specks of light. Then they are fairies. They have all the ease and grace of butterflies delicately opening and closing their wings in the sunlight.

Ping is hovering close by, taking care of me rather than becoming involved with the activity on the hill. I watch, utterly bewitched by the magic of this other realm, which is both within and outside our own.

Gradually, the elves begin to fade away, becoming light, only to reappear as though nothing has happened. The effect is disconcerting, but it does not seem unnatural. By now, my impression is that most of the elves are consumed in light, and they begin an intricate dance, weaving among each other in an ever-changing pattern of flexible lines. No longer following the contours of the hill, they create the impression of a multidimensional dance of light. A line of light simply winks away to appear at some other point, continuing the beautiful pattern of dance. Above this structured dance of total freedom, myriad tiny fairy lights are swirling at tremendous speed in an ordered part of this complex interweaving of energies.

Ten of the elves have retained their classic elf shape, and now, in front of Ping and me, they clasp hands to form a ring.

"They want you to stand in the circle," says Ping encouragingly.

"Do I have to do anything?" I whisper.

Ping chuckles. "Not really. Being involved is doing."

Light as a feather, I step forward. The circle opens to allow me entry and then closes around me. Gradually, the bodies of the elves brighten, becoming lighter and lighter until their forms are lost to some powerful inner illumination. Slowly yet steadily, the circle of light is closing in on me until it touches . . . and I see anew.

A faint shimmering ray of violet-pink light is pouring down from the sky, bathing the hill on which I stand. In some strange way, I can see that this light is composed of minute particles of color, infinitely tiny. They swirl ceaselessly, involved in the same order of movement that is the Nature Spirits' dance. I am aware that this outpouring is endlessly absorbed by the Earth, a source of continuous energy.

I have the impression of tiny, random flakes of snow in the center of this swirling light, caught as though by some inner breeze at odds with the ordered pattern of natural energy. Faintly, the haunting sound of distant wind chimes rings across the hill. Then, in a manner defying all logic and reason, the flakes of snow-light come together as Pan.

He looks at me and smiles, and within that smile is more love than I ever knew was possible. Love beyond human comprehension washes over me, bathing me in sheer goodness. Only in essence is he the same Pan who visits me in our physical reality. He *is* the violet-pink light, the energy of Earth, the Spirit of Nature.

"Do you recognize your surroundings?" His voice is within me, crystal clear and unmistakably Pan.

"No, I don't. Should I?"

"This is the little mountain on which you live. A far more in-depth view to be sure, but the same locality expressing the same energies."

"Good heavens!"

Pan gives a hollow laugh. "I like that. Heaven it is, providing you can see it. Equally, Earth is heaven, here and now, if you can accept that reality."

"How do I do that?"

"Know who you are."

"Oh! Who am I?"

"No one can be told who they are. It is an experience, a shift in reality, a change in consciousness. The dolphin told you who you are, but until you are that Greater Self you cannot know it." He chuckled. "The irony of truth. Who you are encompasses all you are now experiencing, but this is under my influence. When you become that Greater Self, you will know this is who you have always been."

"Is this why Treenie and I moved here? Because of the mountain?"

"There is no single factor. This is *your* place to be at this time. There is no more a single *reason* for anything than there is a single reality. Life is like the multifaceted crystal you experienced in the plateau. Each facet comprises the whole, yet the human view of life is but a single facet. Know the crystal as a whole, and you know who you are."

"It's very difficult. I have been through the experiences of Nature as you required of me, but I still don't know who I am in the way you speak of. What more is there?"

"The facets of Self."

"How am I supposed to come to grips with . . . me?"

Wind chimes peal delightful laughter into the silence.

"In your inimitable manner, I am sure you will manage."

Sadly, wind chimes are the only sound remaining as the whole scene around me slowly fades away. Only as it fades do I realize that a faint, hauntingly beautiful sound has been permeating everything I have experienced. It is so alien a sound, yet so familiar, that I hear it only as it ceases

161

to be—or, to be accurate, when I am no longer able to encompass it. As I am compelled toward a dense physical reality, so I lose the sound of foreverness.

Everything disappears. All too soon only Ping remains, and I feel desperately sad—sad because nothing has changed. All that unheralded wonder is continuing forever, but I am expelled by the nature of my physical reality. It is beyond my reach.

"And there you have it!"

Even as Ping speaks into my mind, I realize my own thoughts. I am not really expelled, even though the reality is nonphysical. One of the purposes of this journey into Nature is for me to learn of other realities and be comfortable with them. "Is all this what life is really about?" I ask Ping.

"Yes and no. This is one reality of life, not *the* reality. And incidentally, it is not beyond your reach. Your purpose on Earth embraces what you just experienced."

"What *is* my purpose on Earth?"

Ping materializes as the classic elf, hovering a few inches above the ground. "It will only have meaning or value if *you* find your purpose."

I give up on the subject!

Ping accompanies me, and again I perceive the forest of trees as I first had, as a column of light and color both containing and contained by the physical tree.

"Can I give you some advice?" asks Ping.

I turn to him eagerly. "You most certainly can."

"Try to hold the realization in your mind that everything you can see around you is *you*. Nothing is not you. Nothing is separate from you. When you plant a shrub, or pick a flower, it is you—totally, absolutely you. You in a different form, another disguise, but you."

I am impressed by Ping's sincerity and power. Each *you* is laced with emphasis, as though to punch the ideas into my psyche.

Ping vanished, and with him went all metaphysical reality. Tears trickled down my cheeks as I stared blindly at the stark physical beauty of the surrounding trees. I had never in my life felt so blind, so numb, so entombed, so dense.

I sat for a long time, trying to come to terms with my normal reality. Gazing at the area where I had so recently experienced euphoria, I tried in vain to recapture the images. I got unsteadily to my feet and walked my heavy body on heavy legs to the very place where violet-pink light had poured—was pouring—into the Earth. I sank to the ground and lay flat, hoping to absorb some of the energy I knew was there.

I gazed up into the sky. This was the most incredible of all that I had experienced. Ping's last words remained with me: "Everything you see around you is *you*." I could believe and understand that now, after all I had experienced in the consciousness of Nature, but Ping's words summed it up. The human consciousness *is* in all life.

Why had Pan propelled me into the realm of Nature Spirits? It could only be to show me, through experience, that this world of ours is not quite as it appears. He wanted to expand my vision, my inner knowing. And, as before, my experience of it became an experience in the whole human consciousness. I also learned that this world of ours is not *only* ours. We not only share it with Nature, we share it with Beings on a dimension out of our physical sight. Then I remembered my artistic friend Kinsley and his drawings of the Nature Spirits. Clearly, some humans can see these dimensions. Where was it all leading? Surely there was nothing left in Nature to experience—except humanity itself!

9
Lost

It took several weeks for me to recover my equilibrium. Each day seemed to be shrouded in clouds. Not even the sun could disperse my sense of loss. The weightiness of physicality was a drag, but normality prevailed, everyday life continued, and gradually the metaphysical impact faded.

Pan was not to be seen, but I had the feeling that he was never very far away. I would have welcomed Ping with open arms, but that little Being was now unavailable.

I spent quite a while discussing the latest "happening" with Treenie. While she was a good listener, as ever, she could not bring the experience back.

Still, her advice was practical. "It seems that a central theme of your experience has been a total involvement in here and now. And it seems very clear that while you are fretting and thinking about it, you are not here and now."

"Yes, I realize that. It's just that—oh, what's the good?"

Time resolved the problem. A few weeks of compulsory involvement in the regular mundane realities of life, and my balance was restored. Once again I could appreciate Nature on her physical terms, but now there was a difference. There's no way I could have lived through that metaphysical experience without my ways of seeing and relating to physical life being changed. My ability to perceive the invisible beyond the visible was becoming activated and enhanced. I now knew that when I listened to the silent voices of Nature, the intelligence I sensed was not abstract. Beings of another reality were the architects of form, the builders of our physical Nature. One of the insights I had gained came with hindsight. When I had witnessed the supernatural dance of the Nature Beings, I had felt the vaguest twinge of familiarity. Later, when thinking about it, the association became clear. The dance had taken the shape and form of the double-spiraled helix of the DNA. I now knew that beyond DNA there was intelligence of an order that would never submit to a physical inquiry. I would have to use more than my intellect. In my journey toward true Self, I would have to learn through doing and being, by knowing through not knowing, as the dolphins did!

Planning and planting a new garden on top of our small mountain near the ocean was pure pleasure. For the next few months, I buried myself in it, lugging ironstone boulders around to suit Treenie's and my taste in landscaping. The open forest I left strictly alone, complete with undergrowth, fallen trees, and rotten hollow logs. There were also several species of native orchids and wildflowers to enjoy where we found them.

Gradually, I grew to love our new home. I now felt connected with the Spirit of the mountain, at ease within some extrasensory aspect of Nature that increasingly imbued me. Despite our intuition that this was *our* place when Treenie and I first set foot on this mountain, it had taken me several months to release the river and embrace the mountain. Although I felt a greater connection with Nature than ever before, I was now far less attached. My relationship with the land was deeper, yet without the roots, and balanced.

Still, during Pan's prolonged absence, I felt an ever-growing sense that I was not doing something I should be doing. I began to feel restless, longing for the kind of action he had made available to me. But the months passed, and nothing! Finally, I decided to go it alone. I gave the matter a lot of thought, trying to determine just where, how, and when I could go. Under Pan's guidance, there had always been a destination and a purpose, plus the security of knowing—or hoping—he would bail me out if things got too rough. Now I was on my own.

But I could come up with no goal that seemed like an inner imperative. Finally, I pushed myself to my limit, and a new idea dawned. Suppose I was now ready for the Guidestone. Suppose I tried to discover my Greater Self on my own. Surely then I could pass through the Door into Beyond. Suppose I initiated my own initiation.

The idea excited me. There were no answers to my suppositions. I simply had to try to find out for myself.

I had to admit that the prospect of going it alone frightened me. My only journey into the Guidestone had been nerve-wracking, and I did not want to repeat it. I procrastinated for another month, hoping that Pan would appear and take control. He did not. I then spent a week trying to convince myself not to experiment with things I didn't understand, but I remained unconvinced. During this time, I immersed the Guidestone in a bucket of fresh rainwater for a couple of days and set it in the full sun to get charged as I had before. I even looked for the little mustard-seed hole, but in vain. Physically, it did not exist.

The inevitable moment arrived. I waited until Treenie was out shopping, took the Guidestone onto the point where I had seen violet-pink light pour into the Earth (I figured I might as well choose a safe place), and sat down comfortably with my back resting against a friendly boulder.

For a while I stared at the Guidestone, half hoping I would get switched off and drawn out as before, but not really believing or even wanting that to happen. The stone sat on a tiny mound about a yard in front of me, as innocent as any of the many rocks scattered about the mountain, but distinguished by its honey color and egg shape. Half an hour passed, and nothing happened. Determined that it was now or never, I jumped up vigorously and leaped skyward before collapsing back to my seat. I leaped up and down until I was exhausted, and still remained totally earthbound, so I gave up in sheer disgust. After ten minutes of frantic leaping, my lungs were panting and wheezing like a pair of ancient bellows.

Soon, when I was breathing at a normal rate, I lay back on the grass, deliberately dismissing the problem and relaxing. I simply watched the leaves on the gum trees gently swaying in a caressing breeze and became blank, emptied of thought, as I relaxed. Without any intent, my mind's eye conjured up the inner chamber of the Guidestone . . . and, with a total absence of effort, I was again in that vast interior.

I am surrounded by the flames without heat and, as a whispering background chant, the endless litany of *"run, run, run."* This time, I am unafraid. Walking forward with a firm tread, I move deeper into the colossal chamber, seeking the massive Doors that previously challenged me. I can feel the presence of the Keeper of the Door, but it is no longer a threat. I feel no menace, only a keen awareness of my presence. After what seems a long time, during which I walk farther into the chamber, I begin to wonder if the Doors still exist. I stop several times, peering into the softly illuminated chamber immediately around me. The flames, which are continual, provide the light, but they also block from my vision anything else that might be of interest. I have no choice but to persevere. The uncomfortable thought that I do not know how to get out of here assails me, but I dismiss it, intending only to go forward into Beyond.

It seems I walk forever, yet I feel no fatigue. Despite the paradox, I am aware of the passing of an enormous amount of time in this state of timelessness. I cannot explain this; it just is! It feels as if years could be passing while I walk, but the time may have been mere seconds.

As I continue doggedly on, the flames grow taller around me. For some reason, I feel encouraged by this, and it is without surprise that I eventually see the vast Doors looming before me.

They are closed, but, as before, I place one hand on each Door at the center and push. They open as softly and smoothly as the passing of a dragonfly.

Before me, in pristine beauty, I see another Earth spinning in orbit—our planet Earth. I have only to pass through the open Doors to go Beyond.

Gingerly, I put one hand out before me, and, as before, I encounter resistance. Although I do not have a physical heart in this mystic place, I can feel my heart pounding. I push hard against the resistance, but it is useless. The harder I push, the greater is the resistance. This gives me an idea. Turning around to face into the chamber, I stand nonchalantly for a while, before casually leaning back against the invisible membrane. Grrr! Scrap one good idea!

I try everything I can think of to get through that open Door. I try crawling, jumping, wriggling, even an apprehensive rush to bash my way through, but nothing works.

I'm beaten, and that insidious, unwanted thought comes creeping back into my mind like a horrid worm: how do I get out of here? I do not know where or how I came in at the back, and I cannot get out the front Door!

As I mull this over, I become aware of a malignant energy close by, and a chill of anxiety sweeps over me. I peer around, trying to see beyond the flames, when with devastating abruptness the flames die down to a few flickering inches. My anxiety climbs higher.

Following a new thrust of hope, I begin to walk alongside one of the huge Doors, hoping to find some salvation where it meets the wall of the chamber. I have an uncomfortable feeling that my reasoning is faulty, but doing something, anything, is better than doing nothing.

Within a few paces, the malignant chill intensifies, and I peer cautiously ahead. Wrapped in living gloom, I see an old witch, and she is staring at me. Her eyes are cold

fire, utterly evil. Horrified, I gasp in sheer terror and, turning, I run blindly, frantic to get away.

A sudden blast of cold heat washes over me and I am
spinning over and over in utter blackness, sobbing in hor-
ror. I float, aware of the evil presence of the crone, but
I am no longer able to run. I drift in no-place, lost in some
awful dimension of desolation and isolation.

Centuries or seconds pass, I have no way of knowing,
but the terrifying, unrelieved darkness is giving way to a
gray-white gloom. Much of my terror has been sobbed away
and, although I am frightened by the presence of the old
crone, she is no longer in my immediate vicinity.

Gradually at first, and then with a rapidly increasing and
undeniable strength, I am gathered up and hurled into a
large, elegantly furnished room.

I am a sixteen-year-old girl, tall for my age, with long
blonde tresses reaching down my back. I am unhappy, in
pain, and dying. My name is Jandine, and I was born with
a deep and passionate desire to sing. Singing is my love
and my life, my one ambition. Can you imagine the devas-
tation I faced on my fifteenth birthday when my father forbade me to sing? He gave me a long lecture on how a family
of our wealth and social standing could not possibly tolerate
such a low-bred activity. He told me he would lose his position and standing of favor with the king if I so demeaned
myself. He forbade me on threat of banning me not only
from my family but from my country as well. That I could
not face. I appealed to my mother for help, but she is weak.
He dominates her ruthlessly and, much as I hate to admit
it, she is no more than his pampered lady in court.

At one stage, I even threatened to ask the king's permission to sing at court, but my father beat me and kept me locked up until I promised I would not disgrace him so. He has always been a remote figure, seldom giving, mostly denying, yet until this I loved my father. Now I hate him. My mother I despise. How could such weakness be so greatly rewarded in life? She is a despicable creature, and I know she dislikes me intensely. I think it is because I am so much stronger than she. She avoids me, although her reason for avoiding me has changed. Once it was because she feared my anger when we clashed, which was often; now it is because she cannot face me.

I slowly draw aside the silk scarf that is wrapped around my neck, and I look again at the terrible growth that is revealed. It is as though a clenched fist is being forced through my neck, pushing out from my throat. It is red, angry, and malignant. I fear it, for I know that I am dying. I do not fear death too badly; I have had time to come to terms with it. But I am sad because many of my hopes and dreams will remain unfulfilled. When I used to sing, lost in an inner joy, I would feel a deep inner knowing, almost as though an inner me was trying to tell me something. I have the feeling that I am more than merely mortal, but I do not know with whom I can safely discuss such sacrilegious thoughts. Such speculation has long interested me. It is ironic that I will soon have the opportunity to learn if I have an immortal Self that can survive beyond death. Sometimes in my deepest, most disturbed dreams, I see an old woman coming toward me. She has terrible eyes that sear my very soul, and I wake up screaming. I know that she is death.

One day, feeling sick and shaky, I decide to go to the temple and pray for help. When the carriage comes around to my door, I notice that the footman cringes back, as though afraid I may contaminate him. I can forgive him, for, much as I hate it, my breath is becoming putrid as the growth eats deeper into my flesh.

Entering the tall, fluted doors of the temple, I feel, along with guilt at my long absence, a breath of cool freshness. Since the growth took hold, my sanctuary has been a dell in the thick oak woods of my father's estate. There, I used to sing, unheard and unhindered, with only the birds and beasts of the woods to hear me. I say used to, for I can no longer sing at all. As my voice fades, so does my health. I am sad; I have many regrets. If only my mother had been able to give me a sister or brother, things might have been different, but she could not. When I was younger I overheard one of the servants describe her as barren as a clay bat. It took years before I understood her remark.

I walk deeper into the coolness of the temple, approaching the altar. There is no one else present, and I feel grateful as I kneel down to pray. I am so thin now, my knees are little more than bone. For months I have lived on a thin gruel, unable to swallow anything of substance. I have felt the presence of that woman of death lately, but I am no longer frightened. Death is inevitable, and I accept that . . . even welcome it, though I do not know what to expect. I can only hope that my thoughts and deepest feelings may be based on truth. If I have a Self that can survive death, then it is possible that I could live again in some other body. This is what I pray for.

174

The walk to the altar has drained what little energy I have, and I feel shaky on my knees. A hand gently grips my shoulder, startling me, and the robed figure of a traveling sage kneels at my side, supporting me. I am weary and grateful, and my head rests on his shoulder, my hand automatically fluttering toward my silk scarf to ensure that my throat is covered.

With a gentleness I have never before encountered, the sage takes my hand in one of his, and with his other hand draws my scarf from my throat. He ignores my weak protests, and, to my shocked astonishment, he bows his head and kisses me on my throat. He kisses me directly on the growth.

Something wonderful is happening. I can feel a warmth spreading through my body, delicious relaxation and peace far beyond anything in my experience—and I am floating, floating, floating.

I am aware of my self floating, slightly shaken by the way I have just died. How I love that unknown sage as I drift in no-place, nowhere at all, in no-time. I realize with an inner glow that I *have* survived death.

I am floating, drifting in timeless space, surrounded and contained in pale light. Drifting, falling, turning over and over . . . frightened . . . falling . . . toward trees . . . a man . . .

I hurry through the deep woods toward my home feeling rather pleased. My name is Joaquín. Beneath my arm, in a bundle of moist sacking, I carry six new plants, all unknown to science. I am scowling and automatically clutch at my neck. Scientists! What do they know? Pompous, stuffed-up idiots standing together in an elite, ignorant group. I seethe with rage as my thoughts follow a familiar track, my fingers tightening their grip on my neck. I was born with a twisted neck and distorted features. A large hump of gristly flesh straddles my shoulders and, I confess, I am not pretty to see.

My parents were not deterred by my physical problem, and the tutor they employed declared that I was a brilliant scholar. Since then, I have advanced the study of botany immensely, yet I remain unacknowledged, unrecognized. Instead, I am considered a freak!

During the past few years, I pushed back the limits on human knowledge of Nature. I have discovered that I contain the ability to communicate with Nature. It has crossed my mind that God may have wished to compensate me for my handicap. Recently, thoughts, ideas, and concepts regarding Nature have flowed into my mind, and my experiments have confirmed them. That Nature is an expression of intelligence I no longer doubt, yet such speculation is considered blasphemy. Nature has taught me that I am immortal, as is all humanity. Sometimes when I am being ridiculed I wish immortality were mine exclusively! I am now embarking on studies to find a way to prove that each separate human is part of one whole consciousness, including Nature, yet I suspect it will be a waste of time. It will gain me even more ridicule. I am almost certain that we each have—or are—a Greater Self, but to discover this part of our normal everyday self requires total dedication. This is why I probably will never prove my theory.

I have shared my insights with a few friends, and the meetings I now attend to discuss my ideas have become quite crowded. This pleases me, for it is a measure of acceptance.

Passing from beneath the huge trees that surround my home, I enter my house. Shock! Half a dozen soldiers are waiting, and they roughly seize me. The contents of my house are smashed and scattered, my botanical experiments strewn about and wrecked.

I have been imprisoned for more than a month, and there is no hope. I have been tortured into confessing that I am a sorcerer, and I am bleeding and broken. My legs have been disjointed, my arms broken, and my face mutilated. Today I face the prospect of one last session of torture, designed to implicate my very few friends, but this I will not do. This session will be the last because today I will die. My deformity has brought me a life of ridicule and rejection. The few dear friends I have shall not suffer for their love and acceptance.

I lie secured on a rack and slowly I am being stretched. Intense pain is searing my body like fire. Amazingly, an old crone stands in the corner watching the torture. She frightens me more than anything they can do. They engender pain; she engenders fear. She alone threatens my feelings of life after death—and no physical torture could be worse than *nothing* after death. Her eyes blaze with an unholy fire and, as the pain reaches an unendurable crescendo, I fall, spinning slowly, into pale, gray light.

Floating, drifting, pain ending, healing . . . I have survived. I was right, there is life after death, but who am I? I am Jandine . . . No, I am Joaquín . . . or . . . am I? Floating, drifting, hovering in a mist of subdued light, images flicker and flash in my mind. I am falling, falling toward those images that I see . . . falling . . .

I cry weakly, fatigued and distressed as I stare up at the palm fronds waving from the tops of long, supple trunks. I am a tiny black child, helpless, abandoned before I can even walk. I am exhausted, thirsty, and hungry, my stomach distended. I have lain for three days beneath the palms, and my time is ending. Maggots are crawling and spilling from the huge weeping sores that cover my body, and I ache from shivering.

I stare up into the palm fronds, and, as I gaze at them, they gradually fade away and I am falling into light. I am floating, floating, wondering who the child was? Was that me? Who is me? I am confused. Am I Joaquín? Who is Jandine? I am lost. Where am I? Who am I? I *must* be someone, but who?

I am drifting. Images flicker before me; I see an image of a man . . .

This time, the crowds listen. Turning them from their pious and piteous belief about God is not easy, but they listen. They listen to my passion as much as to my words, and that is good. People do not want to release their concept of God. They cling, unreasoning, blind but unrelenting.

It terrifies them that God is judgmental, to be feared, yet this is their belief. I speak of a God of love, a God of compassion, and they murmur of heresy. Do I not teach what Jesus taught? I sigh. Look what happened to him!

If there is anything I fear, it is torture—and yet each day I court the possibility.

I wish I could speak of God in total truth, instead of behind veils of insinuation. God is in *all* life, in *all* things. This I know. Heaven is a state of Being, not a place for so-called good people to go. I am a pantheist, but pantheism is considered devil worship, so I speak half-truths and disguise the issue. How I would like to speak of my quest for the Greater Immortal Self and urge others to join me. Then we could quench our natural thirst for Truth. But sadly, very few humans have this thirst. I try to awaken this in others, but they hunger for more and more possessions, more money, more status. Seldom is there a hunger to seek the God within.

My talk is ended, and I step down from the box from which I have addressed the crowd. The people move back as I pass, for a wandering sage is a figure of mystery. My close friends and traveling companions surround me, offering gentle blessings to those we push through as we make our way back to our inn.

I pass through a hundred small towns and villages, speaking, with an ever-growing passion, of God. Discontent with blind faith and the fear of God are spreading, for people are weakened by fear. I offer the strength of love and the forgiveness of God, and the crowds respond. Increasingly, I am hounded and harried by the churches, for their hold on the people is threatened. Often I weep, for those who want freedom, who want love, are punished. We are controlled by fear, separated and isolated from true faith.

In another town, larger this time, people gather in the

hundreds. I am warned that there might be trouble. There is an undercurrent of resistance engendered by the churches. There are arrests, and this frightens me, but I cannot stop. I dreamed last night of arrest and torture. In my dream a voice said, "Michael, Michael, do not break. Your time is drawing to a close and you will be tested. Know your own faith. Whatever wounds you suffer, I will heal. If you will endure, I am truly your God."

It is inevitable. I have no wife or children to mourn me, but I am sad. I have a haunting fear, beyond all normal fear, of torture.

Before I finish speaking to the crowds, I am approached by some priests and denounced as being in league with the devil. I am arrested and imprisoned for heresy.

It crosses my mind that these prison walls are not dissimilar to the walls men build around themselves. I can see mine and know that I am forcibly contained. Am I worse off than those who do not see their constraints and do not know they are imprisoned?

Tomorrow I am to be placed on the rack. I have a choice. I can denounce my teachings, confessing a relationship with the devil, and die, or I can hold to my love, confessing nothing—and die! That death is inevitable I do not question, but my fear threatens to choke me. Why should my fear be so great? Do I fear they will break my spirit? Some of the angel's words come back to me: "Michael, do not break. You will be tested. Know your own faith. Whatever wounds you suffer, I will heal. You will endure." I give thanks for such blessed comfort, but it does not allay my fear. I will try to hold out. Is God testing my own faith?

Have I been tortured to death in some previous life? Is this why my fear is a tangible force? I am sweating as, one by one, the last hours of my mortal life pass by.

I am strapped into the rack. I have the crazy feeling I have been here before, that I have died on the rack, but it must be that fear is causing hallucinations. My mind is wandering from the pressure of fear.

As the tension on my limbs is increased, the pain in my lower spine grows steadily greater. I am blinded by sweat, while every pore of my naked body is running water. Urine is splashing my thighs, and my bowels erupt as a blinding bolt of agony lances through my body. My brain is boiling, but clearly I feel and hear the parting of my spine. Through an open, agonized, distended jaw, I scream, *"God is looooove,"* and collapse into a smothering white light of total peace.

No pain. I am healed. I live. I see images leaping from the subdued light in which I drift. I see a prison cell, the huge blocks of stone remorseless and implacable, and I am falling with dread toward pain. . . .

Sweat is stinging my eyes, caked into the filth congealed on my body. The throbbing pulse in my hands is beyond belief, my groan prolonged and feral. I am a small, lithe, young man; my clothes are in tatters. There is blood smeared over my face and on my garments. I am sitting on a heap of filthy, lice-infested straw. The gloom around me is malignant.

I rock back and forth, holding my fingers in my mouth while I moan.

I am a pickpocket, and the judge ordered that my tools

of trade be removed. They tore out my fingernails, one by one, laughing! Only my thumbnails were spared.

A couple of days pass in a blur of utter misery. I cannot eat, and the sickening offal that is thrown into my cell would offend a dog. Suddenly, there is a voice, and the cell door opens with a creak. "You're free. Get out."

I wander the streets of London, and the cobbles that were once so friendly now jar my body with each uneven step I take. Unintentionally, I blunder into a dockside area, a foul and dangerous place I have always avoided. I look at my blood-caked hands and decide to wash them at the water's edge. I need to see how badly damaged they are, although I know that they will never again settle light as a fly on a lady's purse.

With some effort, I reach the boarded edge of a rotting quay, and I kneel down, stretching my hands to the water. God! It is cold. I lean out further when, soundlessly, a rotten plank gives way.

I am in the water, struggling weakly in the numbing cold. I grab for the boards, crying out in fresh agony as my mutilated fingers strike against the wood. I cannot grip. Within a few minutes, water floods my mouth as I ineffectually cry out for help. There is no one, but for one brief moment I see again the old crone with eyes of death. It was she who called out as I lifted that last purse.

All is rapidly fading into the awful dreams that plague me so often. I dream that I am a young woman with a terrible growth, that I am dying. Then she is replaced by a hunchback. He is a horrible sight and runs toward me, but as I flee I become a holy man in a prison cell.

I make a last ineffectual grasp at the edge of the jetty, sobbing. As I sink into the water, I realize that the dream came true. My prison cell was the cell in the dream, imprisoning the holy man. Who . . . ? I am drunk as I gulp water, laughing as my body sinks, thick and heavy, in the Thames.

I am drifting. Now I know who I am. I am Darfred. I have just drowned, but who is Michael? Drifting, drifting. Who is Darfred? Who am I? Drifting. Another young man walking along the streets . . . I don't want to be this person . . . No.

Whistling a happy tune, I amble away from the trade houses where my father is doing business. I wander downtown, away from the affluence and wealth into the poorer quarters where there are many beggars. I muse on this odd fact. Beggars gain more in the slums from the poor than they do in the wealthy part of town. Compassion must surely be born from pain and need!

What draws me to these undesirable quarters I am not sure, but I often come here. I seem to have a fascination with beggars. To amuse myself, I sometimes put money in a purse and fasten it to my belt. When I walk the streets of a slum, I wait for that feather-light touch of the pickpocket. Strangely, I can always detect it. I pretend that I do not know, so the thief gets the purse. I don't mind. I am wealthy, and they are poor. I feed many families in this way, and it pleases me. I also give to the children. They know I am a soft touch, but I feel so much compassion for starving children. I cannot bear to see the bloated tummy of a hungry child.

People smile at me in the slum quarter. I am no longer

resented as though I insult their poverty with my wealth. They know my game, and we play it with skill and dignity. I once saw a young girl with a growth on her throat. Without warning, I burst into tears and she ran into the hovel where she lived. Several days later, I dropped a silver coin onto the street when I knew she was looking. I hid around the next corner and waited for her to claim it. She did, and I felt a rush of pleasure.

I cease my aimless whistling when I see a beggar approach whom I have never seen before. Most are familiar to me. He comes directly to me, which is very unusual. He is particularly filthy, yet he is unstooped. There is something very odd about this man, and I watch him with keen interest as he reaches me.

He holds out both hands and, looking me in the eyes, asks, "A coin, D'avid?"

But his eyes! Never have I seen such eyes. The eyes of a beggar are furtive at best and usually they are diseased. But this man's eyes are direct and somehow free. They are the eyes of God, of immortality peering into a mortal world.

I reel back from his eyes, staggered, when he turns, and within moments he is lost among the throngs.

For the following two years, I visit the slums, endlessly searching for this man; I know him to be God. Why he should dress in such a way I do not know. I know nothing about him, but his eyes have ignited me, and my search for God will never, never cease until I find him. Although I am a young man, I have always had a feeling of continuity. I have always felt that life is all One, and that each individual is part of the Whole. I have a strong sense of having lived before, a feeling heightened during moments of great stress.

My parents are distraught by my ceaseless search for the god-man, and they resent the time I spend in the slums. How could they understand? They are wealthy from trading in this large town in northern France. They want to leave the business to me now that I am twenty-one, but this means nothing to me anymore. Once the business was all I lived for, but that was before I saw the man. They reason, they threaten, they plead, but nothing can deter me. I must see the beggar who is God again, so I continue to haunt the slums.

Many think I am mad, and no one (except the little girl with the growth on her throat) has seen the man I describe. I find the girl collapsed in a narrow lane, and as I carry her home, she raves in delirium. But she raves of a beggar with stars in his head . . . and I know.

She dies the next day, but I cannot feel sad. I somehow know she is with her starman.

I am walking once more on my mission of hope when I see a human bundle of rags lying in the gutter. People pass it by, but I cannot. I must help. I kneel beside the body, and it is a man. He looks at me, and it is the one I have been seeking. His eyes have never known nor will they ever know death.

"Why?" I gasp. "Why are you like this? Aren't you God?"

His voice is soft but clear. "I am God as mortal. I am a mirror. To find me, look within yourself. Do this, for it is your destiny."

"But how is it no one else has ever seen you?" I ask in tearful anguish.

"They do not see life. I am life."

His head falls back and he is dead, a clear denial of his words!

Even as I gaze at his peaceful face, I see my error. This is not death; this is withdrawal. He has stepped from his body in the same way I step from my carriage—and with the same ease!

A week later, I enter a monastery. This is known to be the place of God. Here I will find him.

Twenty-four years have passed, and I have never once left this monastery. I have tuberculosis and I am dying. I am not afraid of death, for it is only now, in the last few hours of my life, that I realize the depth of my mistake. God is not contained within monastic walls, nor in any church or dogmatic institution. All those years ago, I saw freedom in a man who demonstrated life, not death or poverty. He appeared to me in a way that contained a message, but I was unable to interpret it. I offered compassion to the poor, and within that I found God. Not knowing I had found God, I dismissed that state of Being that God is and went looking for that which I already was. By looking, I denied the having!

During my years here, I have become certain of the continuity of life. I am aware of having searched for God for many lifetimes. In deep meditation, I have connected with some of those past selves. I was a young woman who died from a tumor in her throat. I have been a scholarly hunchback with a passion divided between botany and the search for Oneness. I have been many people who died miserably, and it seems that this death will not be much of an improvement. But at least I am spared pain. I have detected a common thread among the lives I've lived — the endless search for Self, the search to know the truth of who I am.

Phlegm is hot in my throat and I cough. Despite all those years in a monastic order, I have followed my own path. Yes, I mouthed the words of a monk, but in my heart I spoke to God in my own way. During those long hours of silence, I learned to reach the deepest parts of myself, and it was here I found Michael. He had been a holy man. He — I — lived with and will die in truth. During those moments of profound meditation, I learned that I shall live again as another, different Michael, reincarnating once more into this world. I look forward to my next life, for I have learned much that I can bring to a new physical existence. I now know that the Greater Self is not to be found in separate identities but in the Whole. This knowing will emerge in my next life, and I will know *who I am.*

Coughing shakes my body, and I wipe bloody phlegm from my lips. Weakly, I laugh. What a joke that I looked for God in a grim, austere, loveless monastery! God is *love!*

I lay on a thin straw mattress on a solid board bed. My cell is doorless, one cell in a long, bare corridor of empty, lonely cells. Even when occupied they are bare, for without love a human being has nothing, less than nothing. Coughing out my last few breaths, alone in this bleak place, I am feeling a joy such as I never imagined possible. I am thrilled. For the last hour or so, faintly, as if from a far distant angel, I hear a voice calling, "Miiicchhaaeell, Micchhaaeell," over and over. It confirms all I learned of a future me. I am responding. D'avid seems to have receded, and I am attracted to this ethereal, other Michael.

Without any fear or trauma, I feel myself float gently from my body. I am filled with joy. As I float in pure, shimmering light, the arms of a little girl go around me and I look into her eyes. No growth mars her throat, but her eyes are the eyes of God, and I laugh at the joke. No wonder I could never learn her name! No wonder He could not be found. God reaches us through . . . us!

I float, drifting in peace. Who or where I am I do not know. I am lost but I no longer fear. Am I Jandine, Darfred, or D'avid? I am lost in identities, and I laugh, for I am not afraid. I *am* love . . . and this I know.

"Miicchhaaeell" . . . "Michael."

My body jerked convulsively and I opened my eyes. Treenie knelt at my side, concern and love showing in her face. I opened my arms and engulfed her, holding her for long, long minutes while I cried softly. She said nothing— time enough for that later. She simply held me tight, knowing that was my need.

I cried with the memory of suffering and pain I had endured in other lifetimes. I cried for all my suffering as a whole, and I cried for the suffering of each individual identity as he or she struggled to understand. And I cried because I knew that in every other human Being a similar story of pain and suffering was being endlessly enacted. And my crying was a healing.

10
Going Beyond

We lay together in the soft kangaroo grass. All the identities I had experienced tumbled through my mind.

"Why didn't you shake me out of it?" I whispered unsteadily.

"I didn't dare. It was obvious you were somewhere else and I thought it might be dangerous. I could only call you."

"How long were you calling?"

"Long enough to frighten me."

"*How* long?" I persisted.

"Oh, nearly ten minutes."

"Only minutes!" I echoed in astonishment. "I lived a life in those minutes. I lived a long, boring life of chanting, praying, meditating, and misery. I was cold, forever cold, except in midsummer. Ugh! The coldness of stone is incredible. The only relief was meditation. Only in meditation could I enter states of love . . . and discovery."

I told her about D'avid and his meeting with the beggar who was God and about all the years following.

She listened gravely. "Well, it explains your easy ability to meditate, and your intense dislike of cold. Even your love of conversation."

"Of *course*. All those years of strict, imposed silence. We could speak for only an hour each day. And do you know the greatest tragedy? After a while there was nothing to talk about, nothing to share!"

We walked indoors, and over a succession of cups of tea I told Treenie my story. Each detail was etched with such intensity I flinched as I recalled and told it.

"So many people," she said. "Jandine, Joaquín, a poor little black child, another Michael, poor Darfred, and then D'avid . . . and yet all were you."

I smiled ruefully. "It's rather like a litany of pain. Pain and suffering are the only real connections."

"You know better than that. The real connection is the spiritual one. You *were* those other people. Every one of us shares the same truth. Every human being on this planet is an individual who in some way is the total, or an aspect, of all the identities he has ever been. And within all that is the Greater Self, that part of us that is the total, the Whole of who we are." She became excited. "Don't you see! The Greater Self can't be found in a single identity, so looking within must mean looking within the whole, not at a single collection of thoughts." She stared at me expectantly.

"You're right. I know that my search for the Greater Self has lasted many lifetimes. I've just experienced a few of them. Some of the connections are startling, yet they shouldn't be. That other Michael, the wandering holy man, he was a pantheist. So am I. We share the belief that God is within *All*, rather than being a separate deity. But beliefs aren't all that are shared. The very place where that other Michael felt his spine break is where I get my lower back pain. And poor Darfred's fingers. I have bitten my finger-nails since I was a child, and even when I stopped my fingers just go to my mouth—but never my thumbnails! There's more than habit involved. It would seem that my fingers need to be loved and reassured that they are safe. Our consciousness is even within the cellular structure of our bodies, and it carries its own memories. Can you imagine how many people are crippled or deformed as a result of something so shocking in their past that it impressed itself into their bodily consciousness? I seem to remember Pan telling me that anything unresolved in the past remains unresolved in the present."

"Give me a summary of the main connections of your various experiences," Treenie said. "Perhaps then we might find a vital clue that will help reveal the truth of Self. I'm interested in this for me, because *the Truth* is true for everybody. We may differ in our beliefs as individuals, but the Truth of Self is universal."

"That's a tall order." I gave it some thought. "Well, the first thing that comes to mind involves the dolphin experience. I learned that the dolphin experiences a number of identities in each life, while we humans, of course, experience only one. But we do experience a number of identities in a series of lives. The only trouble is, the lives *appear* separate. In truth, the total is one *whole* life. So our way is different from the dolphin way, but it achieves the same result. We try to sort through those many identities and learn who we are. The joke is that we're none of them but we're *all* of them. That much I learned. I knew all this intellectually, but it wasn't my reality.

"The dolphin also told me that while humans are an immortal expression of Divine Love, our identities are brief expressions of human individuality." My eyebrows arched. "Well, at least I know the reality of that now. I've just lived it!"

I did another spell of thinking. "Except for my experiences in the Guidestone, the Door to Beyond hasn't featured in what I have been learning. The Door obviously has a key, like any other door. However, the key to this Door is unique. I'm certain that the key to the Door is the consciousness of self-realization, of knowing *who I am*. In other words, the key is a state of Being. Anything less, and that membrane will not yield. It's not what we know that's required, it's what we *are!*"

"I agree with all that," Treenie replied. "When you consider that the Door is the threshold to other realities, it would seem likely that consciousness is the key. A certain vibration of human love probably vibrates with that invisible membrane."

I nodded. "Beautifully put."

"What else comes to mind?" Treenie asked.

"I think each experience in the mystical realm of Nature is a lesson in the way life works on Earth. Each of my experiences seems to have been a preparation for the next step. Is it possible that I am now at a stage where I can realize that Greater Self and penetrate the membrane of the Door? I suspect that going Beyond is only now a possibility. Other lives and other times have been a preparation.

"What Pan has in store for me next I can't imagine. One thing that's apparent is that each and every experience connects with the Whole. For example, when Pan took me down from the top of the plateau into the center of the huge crystal, I saw each flickering light as separate. It was only when I allowed my perception to emerge that I knew each light was part of One vast Light. Perhaps that is another way to experience everyday life—to allow reason, intuition, and perception to merge. Maybe these faculties together will create a greater view of our reality than we presently enjoy."

"Anything else?" Treenie encouraged me.

"Yes. The consciousness of water gave me an experience of Oneness, while blackberry consciousness revealed that although physical forms of a single species are separate, they are One in spirit. The blackberry reinforced the water's lesson and extended it into a physical reality. And then there was Ping! Ping's words about seeing myself in all the plant life around me indicated that I am also in every *person*. We all are. Talk about Oneness! Nature and humanity *are* One. We cannot learn about a holistic Nature by excluding humanity, nor about humans by omitting Nature. To find the true Self, we must obviously embrace *all* life."

My thoughts had turned back to that night of the terrible storm, and to the storm Being's final words: "Only by surrendering to the storm may you conquer it."

I felt a surge of exciting insight. I gazed at Treenie, my eyes shining. "The Being in the storm was telling me how to become free. It said, Only by surrendering may you conquer. *Now* I get it! I finally understand. The answer is— let my Greater Self emerge. Let it appear within me by surrendering all attachment to identity. We must become individuals *aware* of the All. We have to *be* the One in All, the All in One." Now I was really excited. "Don't you see? We already *are* what we are looking for! We . . . , we . . . "

I looked beseechingly at Treenie. "I can feel it in my heart, I almost know it, but something is blocking that final leap." I sighed in defeat. "Pan also told me that surrender is a letting go, not something you can force. By giving in, you give to the inner Self. Maybe I need to give in. Not give up, but give in!"

Before I went to bed that night, I had the feeling I would soon be seeing Pan again. I mentioned this to Treenie.

"I felt that also," she said. "I feel that a culmination of events is imminent. I wonder how it will happen."

"Does it worry you?"

"It concerns me, but I don't really worry. I trust the process and I *know* you are in good hands. How about you?"

"No, I'm not worried, although if I thought I had to go through some of the experiences again . . . I would rather not think about it."

A week later, I saw Pan sitting on the rock where an invisible violet-pink ray penetrates the Earth. He looked so physical and solid it was difficult to grasp that this was the same ethereal Being I had encountered there several months earlier.

"I welcome you, Michael."

Was it respect I saw in those golden eyes? I could now gaze into them without threat or fear. God, he was so beautiful! For the first time I actually understood those people of an earlier time who may have encountered him. If one could not accept such unearthly beauty and feel at ease within its aura, then one would have to experience fear and distortion. The demarcations between beauty and beast, love and fear, are within our personal consciousness.

"Hello, Pan. I'm really glad to see you." I hesitated only briefly. "May I hug you?"

Pan came to me, his arms open. Hugging him took my breath away. In hugging him I hugged the sky, the open universe. I hugged the woods of my youth and a wilderness I have yet to encounter. I hugged light and a nonhuman Being within the light. He was both solid and without substance, formed and nebulous. But more than anything he was Love!

"You have done very well."

"I thought you might be angry. I didn't know whether I should go alone or wait for you, but I know now. You maneuvered me, didn't you? You knew what I would try?"

"Of course. I told you once that I know you better than you know yourself. I know the Self you are looking for! What was I supposed to do? Ask you to get lost? Only recently I warned that you did not know what lost was. You chose to ignore my warning. Only by becoming truly lost can you find yourself. Don't you remember the question I once asked you? If you lose yourself, how do you find yourself if you do not know who you are?"

"But I haven't found the Self I'm looking for."

"You did exceptionally well. You found the thread of seeking Self and Wholeness within each identity, and you followed it."

"But if Treenie had not drawn me out, I might have drifted forever in that other place."

"Ah, but she *did* draw you out. This was known. I love you, Michael. I wouldn't abandon you. Although I could not be with you—that is Law—your soul mate could not be denied. Without her, you could never have entered that other place."

198

His eyes danced like twin reflections of the sun. Mischief shone from them as transparently as from the eyes of a child.

"And you are not angry at being tricked again!"

I smiled at him. "I seem to have lost my anger—and my fear. When D'avid lost his fear, I lost mine, which isn't surprising considering we are both the same Being. Losing my fear has been rather like losing the dragging weight of a huge anchor. I feel *lighter!* But, one last question. Who is the old witch? She was an evil presence in so many lives. Who is she?"

"I have only one answer to that. We must enter the Guidestone together."

"I don't have the Guidestone out here. It's indoors."

"We don't need its physical presence. Your consciousness contains the Guidestone, just as you are contained by it. You need only relax, visualize the interior, and we are there."

"Relax! That's funny. Did you see me jumping up and down trying to get into the stone? It must have looked like I was throwing a fit." I laughed at the memory.

"No, I didn't see you. I was in another reality."

"Well," I continued, "it was only when I stopped trying that it happened. An image of the chamber in the Guidestone came into my mind, and without struggle I was there!"

"Michael, you have just summarized the art of life. Humans can achieve many of the things they struggle for merely by relaxing. We are talking again about surrender. Focus on what you want to achieve, and then relax. This does not mean that you do nothing; it means you allow the achieving to unfold as a result of your focusing ability. Focus creates the result."

"That's exactly what happened! I take it that you can find your own way into the Guidestone. Or do I visualize us both in?"

Pan laughed, wind chimes and happiness.

"Whichever."

I lay back on the soft grass and relaxed, eyes closed. I felt no sense of urgency. Pan lived in no-time, so there could be no wait. What luxury! For a while I concentrated on the harsh calls of some distant currawongs, relaxing, letting go.

Once again, without effort, an image of the chamber in the Guidestone flowed easily into my mind, and I was there.

I look around, very pleased. I am standing before the Doors, and they are open. Pan is waiting on the other side — in the Beyond — and, walking on air, he comes through the Doors toward me.

"Can I walk through the Doors?"

"Try it."

With my hands out before me, I advance a step, only to meet the familiar resistance. I shrug. "Nothing's changed."

"In reality, much has changed."

"I still cannot enter Beyond."

"Are you sure you really want to?"

"Very sure. After all I've been through? Definitely!"

"Nervous?"

"You know I'm not. Well, just a bit apprehensive. I've had some pretty scary times in here. Come to that, nothing nice has happened to me here at all except meeting you! But I guess that makes up for it."

"If you have any residual fear, tell me now. It's important."

Concentrating on my past states of fear, I grope as deeply as I can into my psyche.

"I am not frightened."

"Why not? It is stupid not to be frightened."

Pan's voice is loud and menacing. I can feel a threat, an unknown power, in his energy. But I am certain. "Because no matter what happens to me, I continue. I don't know who I am, but I do know that my identity is not physical. No matter how bad, how agonizing, physical life may be, I am something more than that—and I will endure."

His voice is a roar, a blast of power. And his face has altered, becoming longer. His horns now embody menace and an aura of evil enshrouds him.

"Are you so sure? Is it not possible that I am the Devil? Humans are so gullible. I may have tricked you!"

It is only now that I really know.

Laughing in his face, I say, "Do your worst, Devil. Gobble me up and spit out all my separate identities."

A naked, sexless, golden Pan regards me. Love and purity radiate with such intensity it seems impossible that evil could ever have existed. Even as the thought comes, I know the truth. Evil does *not* exist. It never has. Ignorance conjures evil from our consciousness and gives it power through our fear.

"You have passed, and I rejoice."

He beckons to me. "Come. Take a look at your old witch woman."

The chamber is illuminated by those white, heatless flames, and I see. Alongside the Door, where I had tried to find a way around it, stands a huge mirror. Looking in, I see my own reflection.

I gasp. What I see is more than a reflection, far more. It is holographic reflection, a perfect three-dimensional image.

"A physical mirror reflects physical reality, but this metaphysical mirror reflects states of consciousness. If your state of consciousness contains fear, fear will be reflected. The old crone was your own fear. It took that form because of an incident in a life long past in subjective time."

"But how? Where did I run?"

Pan points in the opposite direction, to another flawless mirror alongside the other Door. "You ran through the other mirror. A physical mirror can only reflect, but a metaphysical mirror can reflect and absorb."

"Where? Where was I?"

"Exactly where you believed yourself to be. You were in no-time, the space between realities, the all-time."

I turn back to the first mirror, regarding my reflected image with affection. It is only then I realize that the mirror reflects nothing else around me. No flames, not even Pan. Pan?

I spin around, searching, but he is not to be seen. He has soundlessly vanished.

"Paaan. PAAAAAANNNNN." Nothing!

202

But I am not afraid.

I turn back to the mirror, intrigued by the concept of metaphysical reflection. The perfect flawlessness of the mirror is stunning. I reach out and touch the surface of my reflection, snatching my hand away. It is warm, as though alive! In faithful duplication, the mirror reflects my every move, the reflection seeming almost more real than me. I reach out to touch the surface without the imprint of reflection, and there is nothing!

I draw back cautiously. With or without fear, I have no wish to get lost in the mirror again!

I walk to the side of my image, hoping to peer around it and, faithfully, it walks to one side, peering around me. Most perplexing, but why? What is the purpose of this? I turn around, searching once more for Pan, but he is not to be seen. Turning back to the mirror, I recoil in shock. A short, dark-haired girl wearing a dark green dress of some heavy material is staring back at me, her face reflecting astonishment as she recoils from me. Intrigued, I step closer to the mirror, peering into its mysterious depths, and she steps closer to me, peering intently.

I smile and she smiles. I raise my right arm and her right arm is raised. I wriggle my neck and shrug in resignation and she perfectly reflects my actions.

Wow! What a mirror. But who is she? If she is my reflection, is she the *real* me? I am shocked, and my shock registers on her face!

I turn around, facing away from the mirror as I once again look for Pan. "PAAAANN." My shout is smothered by silence. No echoes bounce in this chamber. "Gee, Pan, it just isn't fair. Now what am I supposed to do? Anyway, who is the girl? I've never met her before."

Nothing! No sight or sound of Pan. No response to my attempted conversation.

I turn back to the mirror, deciding to ask the girl who she is. Perhaps this mirror will allow conversation.

Tall and blonde, Jandine stares back at me, her mouth open in astonishment. Another involuntary step back. "Good grief! Jandine!" Her mouth opens and closes soundlessly. Pity. I cannot talk to her . . . me? Stepping closer, I peer at her intently, while she peers at me with equal intensity.

Only slowly, and with great difficulty, am I able to accept the idea that the reflection is myself, not someone else. *I* am the reflection, no matter what reflects.

I gaze pensively at my reflected Jandine, when, with the faintest wisp of movement, the outlines blur, fade, and reform to reveal the exceptional ugliness of Joaquín.

The impact of contrast is considerable. I stand straight, while Joaquín's stance is stooped and twisted. Jandine's throat was unblemished, but poor Joaquín looks as though his neck was twisted by some giant hand when he was a child and he failed to die.

I gaze at him through tear-filled eyes while he stares back with compassion and love.

I ache to hold that broad, squat figure with its unmistakably intelligent eyes, but even as I step helplessly forward, he is changing . . . and a very tall, lean Egyptian is revealed.

Another smart step back! This me looks fierce and arrogant, even ruthless. I feel uncomfortable. I have no recollection of this other me, but I realize that he must be one of the many identities I have forgotten. I step closer, gasping as I see just how tall he is compared to my present body.

I watch and wait. Sure enough, he fades and is replaced by Darfred. I feel I know Darfred well. Looking with interest at his fingers, I see to my surprise that they are healing. This can only mean that my own healing has affected him.

Darfred fades, to be replaced by a small urchin girl, who in turn is replaced by a tiny, helpless black child. Other identities come and go. A Native American stands before me, proud and with immense dignity. My recall is powerful and immediate. After a long life of spiritual development with Nature, I went into the hills to die. By choice I remained bodiless on Earth, moving over the familiar hills and valleys for another century of Earth time. My wisdom and insight into Nature from another dimensional perception revealed the truth of human and Nature as One. Such was the depth of spiritual insight among my people that they knew of me, and I was given a name symbolizing great love and respect. They knew when I passed through their villages, when I helped their dying, and though unseen they would greet me. Never was I feared, for they knew me to be not dead but merely living without a body.

The reflection had faded to be replaced by others, forming and in turn fading. I stare at them, mesmerized. The images are coming faster now. Some cause an immediate emotional response; others are unknown and I cannot respond at all.

Faster and faster, the rapid appearance, consolidation, and fade-outs occur, until I am overwhelmed by identities.

I must get away from this bewildering mirror. I try to turn away but cannot. As long as I watch, neither turning away nor trying to depart, I can move freely, but I am compelled to watch.

A change is taking place within me as, with remorseless purpose, the images come and go. I no longer resist or accept the characters conjured up. I cannot. I am overwhelmed. I cling with despairing energy to the one identity I know I am—Michael, or was it D'avid? No, of course, I am Michael, the heretic sage. No! Who am I really? Abruptly, the images cease. I gaze at . . . nothing. Nothing. *Nothing!* I recoil. Shrinking, shrinking into blackness, endless black density. Dark. Forever, never-ending . . . silence. *All is dark.*

Daaaaaaaaaarrrrrrrrrrkkkk.

A speck of light. In all this total darkness, a minute speck of light. Tiny light, growing . . . growing rapidly. Expanding. *Light. Expanding.* Consuming all dark, devouring black until all is light. All light.

Liiiiiiiiiiigggggghhhhhttt.

Mirror. Metaphysical mirror. Reflection. Human is light! Light of Being. Light of beauty. All light. I . . . I am.

I am *light!* I see light reflected. I see the light of consciousness. This is human consciousness and I realize I am *all* consciousness. I am *all* human. I am One in All, All in One, All in All. Now, finally, I know who I am.

Before me, the mirror is alive with reflected radiance. A light, vaguely shaped in human form, fills the surface. Within this light of consciousness is all I am. I see blackberries creeping over the steep hillsides and hares nibbling the new growth of spring barley. I see a great bronze dragonfly hovering over the cool water of a fresh, clear river, and I see the fish in the river's depths. I see a platypus, my ancient self, and an eagle, hovering against the back-cloth of an endless blue sky. I see beyond the deceptive sky into another familiar world, spinning with silent orbit in a far-distant galaxy.

And there are human Beings. All the identities I have ever believed myself to be gaze back at me. And they smile. I gaze upon my reflected truth. No longer do I see the phys-ical body containing consciousness; it does not. The mirror reveals that consciousness contains the body. In the way a cloud contains the water that will become individual drops of rain, so consciousness enfolds each one of us. And when we become individual, we are still contained within consciousness. Consciousness knows no boundaries; there are none. The consciousness of you and me is One con-sciousness. We are individuals, not separate, within it. If we are hit hard upon the head, we are no longer conscious of consciousness. But there is no unconscious! It is a lie, a hoax. All is consciousness. As we treat each other, so we treat our self. We are One Self. Consciousness is *all*, never separated, never fragmented. Consciousness is *Whole*, forever One.

"Could any Being be told this? It is an experience."

Pan is beside me, radiance sparkling from those golden eyes. I turn to him and find there is nothing to say!

"It can only be an experience. By knowing all selves, you become free of the illusion of self and all with which it identifies. Know also that within this change all the selves you have ever been are changed, for they are not separate from you. The past and the future are a grand illusion."

I smile at him, my heart filled with love. "They are changed because I am changed. We are One. Also, all humanity is affected, for there is no separation between us. Deep within each human psyche, a flame grows brighter, for what affects a part affects the Whole. That is the truth of spirit."

A whole new understanding of life opens before me as I consider it from my new perspective. I like the thought of my past identities experiencing change, however subtle it may be. What a joke! The past is not past. Pan's words of truth have many levels: anything of the past that was unresolved is unresolved now! Equally, what is resolved now is resolved in the past.

My anxieties have vanished. The subconscious imprint that programs our worries is no more. I know that I am not a random collection of genes but an "inspired person." Becoming awake is the birth of purpose.

Glancing pensively at the Door, I am aware that it will now yield to me.

Softly, as though echoing eternally, the words of the Keeper of the Door catch my attention. "To open the Door is to invoke an awesome responsibility. Do not open the Door unless you are prepared to accept this."

Well, I had already opened the Door, even though I had not yet entered.

I accepted the responsibility.

The Keeper's words continue. "If you step into the Beyond, the full force of Nature shall pivot in your Being. Can you accept this enormous responsibility?"

The full force of Nature shall pivot in my Being. Powerful words! I consider them carefully. I am Nature. Nature is within the consciousness that I am. I am changed; I myself am a pivot of change. I accept this!

"Misused . . . it will destroy you."

Even though I am a mortal human being, I am far, far more. I am consciousness. I span the Earth, the universe. And as I am, so is every human Being, but now I know this *profoundly*, not merely intellectually. I cannot misuse the power of Nature. I am that consciousness.

"Well, that takes care of the preliminaries. Now we can wrap up the action." Pan's words are a breath of light, of never-ending humor.

"I'm ready, too." So saying, Treenie stands at my side and reaches out to take my hand.

For long moments, I am speechless. Then I laugh. I ask no questions—after all, this angel does it her way! Together, Pan, Treenie, and I walk through the Door into the waiting mystery of Beyond.

Epilogue

Some considerable time later, after I had written this book of my experiences, I asked Pan if there was anything I could share with you, the reader, that would empower you, or enable you to find the truth of who you are. He smiled at my seriousness. "Within the pages of your book are many truths that apply to all. I am sure they will be recognized."

"Yes, I know that. But I want to offer something that can be used daily, something with tangible value."

"Then I suggest you search your own memory and draw from your own experiences. You, more than I, should be able to encapsulate the knowledge you have gained and make it available."

I walked alone among the tall trees, listening as the breeze whispered among the leaves overhead. Ah! Yes! Here lay one tangible reality. Here was a part of life that eluded most people, as it had me. The art of *listening*, of being in the moment. If we listen, totally, we cannot think, for thinking moves us away from the moment. We can think and hear, but hearing is not listening. Listening brings us into the moment, the only place of life, of God.

Practice listening to the sounds of Nature around you, or, if you live in a city, listen to your favorite music played softly enough that you really have to listen to hear it. When thoughts intrude on your listening, just accept it and, without resistance, let them go. You cannot force listening; you can only surrender your resistance to listening!

As I gazed up at the leaves moving above me, I remembered Pan having asked me if I could see what he was seeing when he and I gazed up into a similar tree. And I had looked in vain. That incident taught me that we are very practiced at "looking at," but not at *seeing*. We look at Nature and people through yesterday's eyes, just as we hear with yesterday's ears. We have forgotten how to see anew, the way a child sees, everything brimming with the excitement of discovery. We have labeled and categorized everything, and we have lost the newness of seeing. Practice seeing your relatives, your family, your life partner, and your closest friends as totally new people every day. Put aside yesterday's images and concepts of who they are, and experience them anew, each day.

Once again, this brings you into the moment, the isness of now. See each familiar flower, tree, and plant as though you were seeing it for the first time. Really *see*. You will find that your relationship with your life partner, your parents, your children, your friends, and Nature will change. It will become more creative, more open, allowing far more room for love. But even more than this, your relationship with yourself will change, for as you see others anew, so will the newness of yourself emerge within you. And within this newness lies the potential of you experiencing who you are.

I sat down, my back against the smooth, comforting trunk of a small gum tree. What else? What other simple, overlooked reality is lost in the claw and rush of daily living? What we see and hear is by far the greatest part of our sensory input, but what other aspect of life lies hidden under separation, habit, and illusion?

Memory conjured up the lesson from Ping. Ah yes! How to practice connecting with life by deliberately defying the illusion of separation. Practice seeing everything around you that has life as you in disguise. Again, this means *you* within your friends, family, loved ones, even those people you dislike, all trees, animals, in fact, all aspects of Nature. If you truly practice pretending that you are everything around you in disguise, eventually you will experience the overwhelming exultation of *knowing* that this is not pretense. Your relationship with life will change positively and dramatically.

I lay back, staring up at the few pale gray clouds scudding across the vast backdrop of space.

It's not much, I thought, and it all seems far too simple, but it is something that can be practiced in everyday life. Simple it may well be; easy it is not! Nevertheless, I know that if these few basic realities are practiced with a focus on becoming aware and awake, then in perfect timing these realities will help to overwhelm the illusions that enfold you. I know that if you accept that "knowing who you are" is possible, and if you have the courage to follow wherever the journey takes you, then nothing can stop you.

About the Author

Michael J. Roads was born in Trumpington, Cambridge, England in 1937. In 1964, he and his wife, Treenie, and two of their children emigrated to Tasmania, Australia, where for the next twelve years Michael was a beef and dairy farmer. During this period, Michael left behind conventional farming methods and switched to organic farming. This move encompassed a dramatic inner change that allowed him to reconnect with nature. During this time, Michael wrote *A Guide to Organic Gardening in Australia,* which was the first book written on the subject in Australia. It was published in 1976.

In 1976, after selling their farm, Michael and Treenie and their four children spent nearly a year traveling throughout Australia and Michael wrote his second book, *A Guide to Organic Living in Australia,* which was published in 1977. Both these books were Australian best-sellers.

In 1977, Michael initiated the Homeland Foundation Community in the Bellingen Valley, an experiment in holistic living modeled on the Findhorn Community in Scotland. Four years later, Michael and his family left the community and lived in a rented house in the Bellingen Valley. For the next two years, Michael practiced as an Organic Farming Consultant.

Eventually, responding to an inner urge, Michael became a full-time writer. From his experiences, Michael wrote *Talking With Nature,* describing an extraordinary journey into the heart and soul of nature, published in the United States in 1987 by H J Kramer Inc. This book has since been published in German, French, Spanish, and Dutch.

Another book on organic gardening, *The Natural Magic of Mulch,* was published in Australia in 1989. This book has been widely acclaimed as a sensitive, informative, and easily understood book on the subject.

In addition to writing full time, Michael is a workshop leader. He gives talks and seminars on the "Spirit of Nature" and with Treenie teaches a seminar called "Becoming Free."

Michael is open to correspondence. The address is:

Michael J. Roads
"Serendipity"
Kiel Mountain Road
Woombye, Qld 4559
Australia

BOOKS THAT TRANSFORM LIVES
FROM H J KRAMER INC

ORIN BOOKS
by Sanaya Roman
The Earth Life Series is a course in learning to live with joy, sense energy, and grow spiritually.

LIVING WITH JOY, BOOK I
"I like this book because it describes the way I feel about so many things."—VIRGINIA SATIR

PERSONAL POWER THROUGH AWARENESS: A GUIDEBOOK FOR SENSITIVE PEOPLE, BOOK II
"Every sentence contains a pearl . . ."—LILIAS FOLAN

SPIRITUAL GROWTH: BEING YOUR HIGHER SELF, BOOK III
Orin teaches how to reach upward to align with the higher energies of the universe, look inward to expand awareness, and reach outward in world service.

JOY IN A WOOLLY COAT: GRIEF SUPPORT FOR PET LOSS
by Julie Adams Church
JOY IN A WOOLLY COAT is about living with, loving, and letting go of treasured animal friends.

EAT FOR HEALTH: A DO-IT-YOURSELF NUTRITION GUIDE FOR SOLVING COMMON MEDICAL PROBLEMS
by William Manahan, M.D.
"Essential reading and an outstanding selection."—LIBRARY JOURNAL

YOU THE HEALER: THE WORLD-FAMOUS SILVA METHOD ON HOW TO HEAL YOURSELF AND OTHERS
by José Silva and Robert B. Stone
YOU THE HEALER is the complete course in the Silva Method healing techniques presented in a do-it-yourself forty-day format.

LOVE AND PEACE THROUGH AFFIRMATION
by Carole Daxter
"Among the leaders in books that inspire and expand human awareness."—COLIN SISSON